HOW TO WORK FROM HOME

How to Apply for a Job
How to Apply to an Industrial Tribunal
How to Be a Freelance Journalist
How to Be a Freelance Secretary
How to Be a Local Councillor
How to Be an Effective School Governor
How to Become an Au Pair
How to Buy & Run a Shop
How to Buy & Run a Small Hotel
How to Choose a Private School
How to Claim State Benefits
How to Communicate at Work
How to Conduct Staff Appraisals
How to Counsel People at Work
How to Do Voluntary Work Abroad
How to Do Your Own Advertising
How to Emigrate
How to Employ & Manage Staff
How to Enjoy Retirement
How to Find Temporary Work Abroad
How to Get a Job Abroad
How to Get a Job in America
How to Get a Job in Australia
How to Get a Job in Europe
How to Get a Job in France
How to Get a Job in Germany
How to Get a Job in Hotels & Catering
How to Get a Job in Travel & Tourism
How to Get into Films & TV
How to Get into Radio
How to Get That Job
How to Help Your Child at School
How to Invest in Stocks & Shares
How to Keep Business Accounts
How to Know Your Rights at Work
How to Know Your Rights: Students
How to Know Your Rights: Teachers
How to Live & Work in America
How to Live & Work in Australia
How to Live & Work in Belgium
How to Live & Work in France
How to Live & Work in Germany
How to Live & Work in Hong Kong
How to Live & Work in Italy
How to Live & Work in Japan
How to Live & Work in New Zealand
How to Live & Work in Portugal
How to Live & Work in Saudi Arabia
How to Live & Work in Spain
How to Live & Work in the Gulf
How to Lose Weight & Keep Fit

How to Make a Wedding Speech
How to Manage a Sales Team
How to Manage Budgets & Cash Flows
How to Manage Computers at Work
How to Manage People at Work
How to Manage Your Career
How to Master Book-Keeping
How to Master Business English
How to Master GCSE Accounts
How to Master Languages
How to Master Public Speaking
How to Pass Exams Without Anxiety
How to Pass That Interview
How to Plan a Wedding
How to Prepare Your Child for School
How to Publish a Book
How to Publish a Newsletter
How to Raise Business Finance
How to Raise Funds & Sponsorship
How to Rent & Buy Property in France
How to Rent & Buy Property in Italy
How to Retire Abroad
How to Return to Work
How to Run a Local Campaign
How to Run a Voluntary Group
How to Sell Your Business
How to Spend a Year Abroad
How to Start a Business from Home
How to Start a New Career
How to Start Word Processing
How to Start Your Own Business
How to Study Abroad
How to Study & Learn
How to Study & Live in Britain
How to Survive at College
How to Survive Divorce
How to Take Care of Your Heart
How to Teach Abroad
How to Travel Round the World
How to Understand Finance at Work
How to Use a Library
How to Work from Home
How to Work in an Office
How to Work with Dogs
How to Write a Press Release
How to Write a Report
How to Write an Assignment
How to Write an Essay
How to Write Business Letters
How to Write for Publication
How to Write for Television

Other titles in preparation

WORK FROM HOME

A practical handbook for the independent professional

Ian Phillipson

Second edition

How To Books

British Library Cataloguing in Publication Data
A catalogue record for this book is available from the British Library.

© Copyright 1992 and 1995 by Ian Phillipson.

Published by How To Books Ltd, Plymbridge House, Estover Road, Plymouth PL6 7PZ, United Kingdom. Tel: Plymouth (01752) 735251/ 695745. Fax: (01752) 695699. Telex: 45635.

First edition 1992
Second edition (revised) 1995

Typeset by PDQ Typesetting, Stoke-on-Trent
Printed and bound by The Cromwell Press, Broughton Gifford, Melksham, Wiltshire.

Contents

Illustrations

Preface
to the Second Edition

The respected Henley Centre for Forecasting estimates that some 15% of the work done in this country by the first few years of the next century will be done 'remotely', that is working *away* from the traditional workplace. Many of these people will be working from home for at least part of their working week.

Improved technology, computers and faxes now allow many professional, creative and business people to switch away from the traditional workplace and yet still keep in touch with colleagues, suppliers and customers.

As their numbers have increased, so the image of homework as being the preserve of people earning pin money from low paid repetitive tasks has changed. Working from home is no longer a 'cottage' industry.

Working from home can make your life easier, but working from home is no easy option. It *really* is not the same as working from a traditional office. For those who think that it is a rude awakening waits. Just because you have mastered life in a large office does not mean that running a small business or office from home will be a breeze. Indeed, many executives or workers from a large corporate structure find it difficult to cope with the demands of homeworking.

But if you would like to be one of the growing numbers who are making a success of their new working lives, this book is for you, and this new addition has been revised and updated to include all the latest information on the subject you may need.

Ian Phillipson

1
Why Work from Home?

SPOKEN FROM EXPERIENCE

'I wish I were Homeward Bound.' Simon and Garfunkel.

'Home isn't where the heart is. It's where I keep my wordprocessor, fax and photocopier.' Steve Meredith, architect.

'Loneliness can be conquered only by those who can bear solitude.' Paul Tillich.

'We are told that talent creates its own opportunities. But... intense desire creates not only its own opportunities, but its own talents.' Eric Hoffier.

A GROWING TREND

Homeworkers need specialist skills to make their business succeed, but to make the most of their new workplace they must also be Jacks and Jills of all trades.

In succession, and often at the same time, they must be secretary, organiser, designer, office trainee, manager, computer expert, psychologist, motivations expert... and their own boss. They must always be willing to learn. They must also be entrepreneurs.

This is not a traditional 'starting up in business book'. There are already many volumes available which tell you how to choose a business, write business plans, keep acounts, understand tax and price your goods, including the highly informative *How to Start a Business from Home* in this series by Graham Jones.

Instead, the purpose of this book is to help you organise your home office, establish routines to keep you productive, solve some of the problems you might encounter and encourage you to present yourself more effectively to the outside world.

Throughout it is assumed that if you are starting your own home business you have sufficient skills to make a go of it. If you do not then you will not survive, unless you are a very, very fast learner. And though this book is aimed primarily at those who run or intend to run their own

IS THIS YOU?

Accountant		Architect
	Artist	
Broker		Business analyst
	Cartoonist	
Charity worker		Clerical worker
	Club official	
Copywriter		Councillor
	Computer programmer	
Creative worker		Desktop publisher
	Designer	
Editor		Event organiser
	Franchisee	
Engineer		Film producer
	Caterer	
Fundraiser		Graphic designer
	Graphologist	
Head hunter		Holiday agent
	Illustrator	
Indexer		Interior designer
	Keyboard operator	
Journalist		Management consultant
	Market researcher	
Photographer		Personnel consultant
	PR consultant	
Publisher		Quantity surveyor
	Researcher	
Sales representative		Software engineer
	Solicitor	
Telesalesperson		Translator
	Video producer	
Word processor		Writer

full-time business, it will help anyone who spends even just a few hours each week working from home.

So, if you fall into one of the following categories *How to Work from Home* should be of use:

1. Do you already work from a home office, but don't think you are being as productive as you could be?

2. Are you looking to set up a business either part or full-time from home, because you are tied to your home or just think it is the most cost-effective option?

3. Are you able to use computers and new communications technology to work from home?

4. Are you a full-time employee who wants to set up another office away from your normal workplace so that you can work at weekends or in the evenings?

5. Are you a voluntary worker or club official who has to spend a number of hours each week at home on administration and the like?

THE ADVANTAGES OF WORKING FROM HOME

As a homeworker you have great opportunities to control a large part of your day-to-day environment. You can add to your personal comfort and generally improve the quality of your life in ways you never can when working from a standard office.

Reduced travel costs

Homeworkers don't commute. Given that the average commuter spends over three hours per week travelling to and from work and the London commuter nearly six working weeks in transit each year, working from home is a godsend.

Just imagine waking up each morning, dressing, pattering down the stairs for a quick bite to eat and a cup of coffee, then two minutes later being at your desk and ready for work!

Without these daily journeys other problems disappear. There are no unpredictable travel delays to stress you. There is no chance of being involved in a commuter-time traffic accident, unless the route between your bedroom and office is a highly unusual one. And there are no travelling costs, so the £3-4,000 or so that commuters on average spend going to and from work can stay in the bank.

Working from home is also environmentally friendly. No more spouting exhaust fumes into the air each morning—and a computer runs for one year on the energy that a commuter uses on just *one* car journey into work!

More control over your working day

To a large degree you are master of your own destiny. You are able to create and act upon your own ideas and decisions. If you do not want to do something then you don't *have to* do it (though this freedom can only be carried so far—try telling the taxman that you don't want to keep any books this year!).

As a homeworker you can control the pace at which you work and the way you shape your day. If traditional nine to five hours don't suit, you simply change them. There is nothing wrong with working from three a.m. to eleven a.m. or even spending twenty-four hours chained to your desk, as long as it doesn't become a habit. You can take breaks when you want them and not when someone else dictates. Of course the degree of flexibility you can achieve depends on your type of work and markets.

Case histories

The novelist

Well into her fourth book, Ursula is now an experienced novelist who apart from a spate of research needs little contact with the daily world. Because of this she is able to work when she is most productive, which is at night. So Ursula keeps the hours of an owl, writing at night, sleeping during the day.

The journalist

On the other hand, Daniel is a freelance journalist. He needs to interview all manner of people, some of them first thing in the morning, others last thing at night, but most during normal business hours. He has to keep his week very flexible, letting it be guided by stories, easing down when news is slow, working all hours when it is breaking.

Working in tele-sales

Stella works in telephone sales. She only contacts the retail trade and because they only work nine to five hours, Stella can only work effectively then. Even if she wanted to start work early or finish late, she can't.

Lower overhead costs

If you set up a home-based business, you can minimise your start-up costs. For one thing there is no expensive office accommodation punching a hole in your bank balance, irrespective of whether you make money or not.

Achieve more

Homeworkers are in general 30-100% more productive than their office-based counterparts. That gives you the choice of working shorter hours or increasing output. If you spend your working week away from home having an office at home lets you extend your 'weekend' but still work effectively on Fridays and Mondays. Important reports and projects that require great concentration can be tackled then without the disturbances of a standard office.

Spend more time with your family
Working from home allows you to be near your family. Young children, parents and the disabled can all benefit from your attentions. However, their demands and presence can be a disadvantage.

Increase your comfort
There is no need for you to buy an expensive 'power-dressing' wardrobe to keep up with Joneses. You can go to work in jeans and T-shirt if that is what makes you feel comfortable.

Increase your opportunities
The very act of commuting into a traditional office tends to reinforce the image you have of yourself. You become more and more of an accountant, manager or programmer. By working from home you're better able to tear off the labels we all stick on ourselves. When you work from home you begin to see other opportunities. The world becomes more of an oyster to explore and less of a straitjacket.

THE DEMANDS AND DRAWBACKS

Working from home does not create the perfect world. As with all other areas of life you only get out of it what you put in. Not everyone is temperamentally suited to working from home and while some people naturally flourish in this environment, others don't. Working from home is really no soft option.

Increased loneliness
While the conventional workplace offers great opportunities for social contact, when you work from home you have few chances to mix with others. The loss of such social chit-chat and gossip should not be underestimated. Those not equipped to deal with this can soon become demoralised. Not surprisingly, a standard complaint of many home-workers, both novice and experienced, is a feeling of 'creeping isolation', as it has been described. Often you will have to work alone for long periods of time.

Lack of help and support
When you work from home, you generally work alone. There is no-one

sitting in the next office whose brains and experience you can tap or take over some of your commitments.

Numerous distractions

The comfortable surroundings of home so near at hand can prove a powerful distraction. Five minutes sitting in front of the television can all too easily stretch into half an hour, all of it wasted work time. The potential for your working day to be disrupted by friendly but serious sources of interruption is a constant problem. While you might bark at an office junior who disturbs your concentration, it is an altogether different matter when that disruption is caused by your four-year-old daughter! Homeworkers who fail to protect their working time from family, friends and pets end up unproductive, disillusioned and frustrated.

Lack of a rigid work day

At home there is no formal structure to create the framework of your day. You decide what you are going to do and when. And after you have done that for today, you must do it for tomorrow, and then again for next week and next month. For those who are used to having their day directed and organised this can be a culture shock.

Increased family tensions

When your house becomes both home and workplace, new tensions can soon be generated between family members, friends and neighbours. Being around people for hours on end, even the ones you love, can turn minor irritations into major problems. For instance, you may expect too much from your partner and family. Women in particular find that others still want them to run the household single-handed on top of their work. If these problems are not recognised and countered at an early stage they can soon develop into real enemies of productivity and comfort, which are after all two of the main advantages of working from home.

Lack of motivation

Not everyone can make the changes needed to work from home effectively. Some people, because of their own personalities or the very nature of their jobs, simply require the stimulation of others. After all, it can be very difficult to keep yourself 'pumped-up' trying to sell on the telephone if you are the only one around. No-one is there to share the glory of your successes while your failures can seem ever more depressing.

DO YOU HAVE WHAT IT TAKES?

To some extent or another you will need all of these abilities to work from home. How many do you have?

- **Self-discipline.** Work time is still work time, even at home and when a job has to be done, you must sit down and do it, no matter if it's not 'quite the right time' or slightly inconvenient. A homeworker must be able to complete jobs alone, without the supervision of someone standing over them.

- **Effective time management.** Without a formal structure time simply can drift away. A homeworker must learn how to use time effectively and plan the day.

- **Dedication.** Working from home is not an easy option. When times are tough, the homeworker needs to be able to keep going, often without the help of others.

- **Confidence.** Homeworkers must be confident in their own abilities. There is no-one else to do the dirty work. It is all down to you. If you don't do the job then it doesn't get done.

- **Communication skills.** Homeworkers must learn how to deal with every sort of person: clients, suppliers, creditors, debtors, bank managers, accountants, printers and so many, many more. This means being professional with everyone. Working from home is certainly *no* excuse for slipshod work or bad manners.

- **Flexibility.** The homeworker will have to cope with a great number of very varied situations. A mind that can quickly turn to take on another job is a valuable asset.

- **Trustworthiness.** Always be honest with yourself. If you don't want to do something, work out why. Never lie to yourself about what you have achieved. It isn't worth it. The problem doesn't go away.

FAMILY CONSIDERATIONS

Before you start work from home it is vitally important to discuss the whole matter with your family. When you are at home all day you will alter the pattern of family life. You should find out their views as soon as possible. If the rest of the family do not give you support and co-operation you will find it very difficult to work successfully from home. For more information on solving family problems see Chapter 9.

Action point
Arrange a family meeting as soon as possible. Discuss the following points:

- What do others see as the advantages/disadvantages of you working from home?

- On balance do others think that you are doing the right thing?
- When you work from home, how will it affect others' lifestyles?
- Can they be involved in your work in any way?
- Do they accept that you might have to work longer hours?

IS YOUR HOME SUITABLE FOR HOMEWORK?

If you are not going to receive suppliers and clients at your house then its location should have little effect. However, if you live in the middle of bleak moorland clients will not be enthusiastic to make a trek to see you.

Should you go out to visit clients a lot, then the nearer you are to a railway station, a good road network, or an airport the more convenient it is. Only you know how much inconvenience you are willing to put up with.

Thankfully in these days of modern communications and high technology, many people can work from home, even if they live in the middle of nowhere. Even remote areas of the Highlands and Islands of Scotland can now provide a working base for 'teleworkers' whose business is conducted on telephone/fax and computer. All the same, teleworkers should be wary of thinking that now they can set up shop in any remote location.

While the technology does exist to let you operate from almost anywhere, you are totally dependent on phone lines. These can be damaged by bad weather and the remoter the area you live in, the longer it takes to locate faults and repair them. The same can be said about your electricity supply.

GETTING UP AND RUNNING

Deciding to work from home, at least part-time and probably full-time, takes careful thought and planning. Though for the redundant and unemployed, the decisions are easier because there are fewer options to be considered, you should still deeply consider the consequences.

Decide to start your business on a specific day and stick to it. Choose a sensible date. Saying that you are going to begin working from home tomorrow is wholly unrealistic. You will need at least a few weeks to sort yourself out.

If your feet are to hit the ground running from Day One, you must begin preparations at least one month before the date you intend to start work from home. If you do not do this then valuable time and momentum will be lost.

Avoid starting work at a time when you have other pressures on you.

(Example of notes from one initial family meeting.)

January 17th, 194X

Issues Raised	Initial Thoughts/Actions
① Long hours mean I won't see very much of the family.	I will try and keep weekends free. I will also keep the family involved with my work so they know what's going on.
② There will be less money coming in at first.	I won't go ahead with working from unless I get some good potential contracts before July.
③ How will Tommy get to school if I'm no longer driving to work in that direction?	I will still take Tommy to school.
④ If you are going to be working from home it means you can do more around the house.	I'm not at home to do housework, but to work. I'd like the co-operation to do that, but I will do as much as I can. We will discuss this at a later meeting

School and bank holidays are not good times. They have great potential for disruption which is the last thing you want when just beginning to work from home.

Case study – Rosemary puts off priorities

After fifteen years working as a researcher, Rosemary was made redundant. This didn't worry her too much as she was sure that there was a market for her services and she was confident of her own abilities. Rosemary decided to start work on her new company on March 17th which was two months away, enough time she thought to take a good holiday, mull over life in general and 'recharge her batteries'.

When March 17th arrived Rosemary had the chance to go shopping with a friend she hadn't seen in ages. She went, telling herself she'd start work the next day, after all what did one more day matter? The next day the car broke down and she had to take it to the garage. What with one thing and another, Rosemary only got down to 'work' on March 23rd.

Now Rosemary had chosen a spare bedroom as an office and was excited by the thought of kitting it out. It was a comfortable room but the colour of the walls was wrong. Rosemary set to work painting them. It took her three days. After this she spent two more days touring shops looking for office furniture. Eventually she ordered a beautiful desk but unfortunately it would take two weeks to arrive. That didn't worry Rosemary too much. She was happy to be 'working' for herself, after all there was so much to be done. In the meantime, she set about designing and ordering letterheads and generally pottering around 'being self-employed'.

Then at last the desk arrived. For the first time Rosemary could really sit down in a room that was beginning to look like her office. It took another five days before everything was to Rosemary's satisfaction and she could make her first telephone call looking for work. The date was April 21st, over one month after Rosemary said she was going to launch her business.

In that time Rosemary had been playing at work, using the fun of buying furniture, dealing with printers and organising her office as a subconscious excuse to put off starting the real business of work!

Self-discipline is not one of Rosemary's strong points. It is doubtful that her business will survive to see its first birthday.

A HOMEWORKER'S CHECKLIST

These questions are primarily aimed at people who intend to work full-time from home. The answers should give a good indication of whether you are suited to homeworking. If you answer mostly 'no' then you may find the demands too great. However, if you have self-discipline you can overcome most obstacles.

- Do you find it relatively easy to work for long periods on your own? When was the last time you had to do this?

- When you have a project or task to do, can you set your own targets and deadlines to meet them? Give an example of when you last did this.

- How well do you plan your time? Did you plan your time today?

- Can you say 'no' to others when they want you to do something that you don't want to do? When was the last time you did this?

- How well do you concentrate? What jobs or activities have you undertaken in the last month that have needed good concentration?

- Can you do unpleasant things when you have to do them without being told by others? What was the last really unpleasant thing you did without someone telling you to do it?

- Can you leave your favourite television programme to do an unpleasant chore if it has to be done? When was the last time you did this?

- If confronted by a niggling problem do you generally try to sort it out yourself before seeking help from someone else? Give an example of your determination to do this.

- You need information but don't immediately know where to find it. Can you generally track down people who are able to help you? What problems have you solved by doing this?

- You promise yourself to do something and then for some reason can't do it. Do you feel guilty? How many times has this happened in the last week?

- You are asked to do a small task that you have never done before. You are told it's easy. Do you treat the job as a stimulating challenge? What challenges have you undertaken in the last month?

- You have a strict timetable for the day but then something happens to change it dramatically. Do you accept that circumstances have changed and that you need to be flexible? When was the last time this happened?

- You promise to finish a project by Thursday though you know nobody will mind if it's delivered Friday. Would you still generally deliver the project on Thursday? Can you list three times when you have done this?

- Can you budget your money carefully? How much money to the nearest £5 is in your bank account?

- Do you generally pay your bills on time?

- Are you tough with people who owe you money? How many people have owed you money for over a month?

- Are you good at keeping records? Could you find your birth certificate, your car's MOT certificate and the last quarter's phone bill in the next two minutes? Try it. Now did you do it in time? Yes ☐ No ☐.

- When you set out to do something do you generally do it? In the last year how many things can you think of that you promised yourself you'd do and then didn't?

- Are you prepared to work seven days on the trot if you have to finish a job? When was the last time that you did more than you were required to so as to finish a job?

- Do you have general secretarial and management skills? If so what are they?

- Are you confident in your own abilities to keep going and overcome tiresome day-to-day knocks? What makes you answer yes?

When you have answered these questions, ask a friend or member of the family if they agree with your self-assessment.

Action points

- List the advantages of working from home for you. Think of as many points as you can.

- Make a similar list of disadvantages. Don't leave out any potential problem no matter how trivial it seems.

- List all the people you know who could help you with your home business. Include your bank manager, accountant, librarian, old business colleagues, family members and especially anyone already working from home.

- Write down the date when you will start organising the basics of your home office and business.

- Write down the date when you will actually begin working from home.

2
Keeping It Legal

SPOKEN FROM EXPERIENCE

'An Englishman's home is his castle.' Proverb.

'It is unfair to believe everything we hear about lawyers—some of it might be true.' Gerald F Lieberman.

'If the law supposes that,' said Mr Bumble, 'the law is an ass—a idiot.' Charles Dickens.

'The big print giveth and the fine print taketh away.' J Fulton Sheen, Roman Catholic Archbishop.

INTRODUCTION

Though it does depend on your type of work, there are few real legal matters that need concern the homeworker. Those of most concern will be whether the planning authorities, your house deeds, or your mortgage company will actually let you work from home in the first place. The information in this chapter is of course only advisory, and any homeworker who is uncertain of their legal position should seek advice from solicitors, accountants and other professional advisers.

PLANNING REGULATIONS

Planning regulations are the one 'legal' area most likely to affect the homeworker. To what extent that will be depends very much upon your business and type of work. In recent years, planning restrictions have been applied in a more relaxed fashion encouraged by Governments that look favourably on entrepreneurs and homeworking, so in general, most homeworkers should have few problems with the planning authorities. The planning system is divided essentially into two parts: **planning permission** and **building regulations**.

What are building regulations?
To ensure that a new building or alterations to an existing one are safe, a

system of detailed building regulations must be complied with and inspectors will visit the site to ensure they are. Building regulations are different from planning permission, and the fact that you are granted one does *not* mean you will be granted the other.

When are building regulations likely to be needed?
For the homeworker, building regulations will apply if you intend to create more office or working space by:

- building an extension (a porch or conservatory built at ground level and under thirty square metres is exempt); or
- making internal alterations that alter the structure of the house (removing a load bearing wall for instance); or
- installing larger windows.

What form do building regulations take?
There are two building regulation procedures which you can choose from; a **Full Plans** application and **Building Notice** application.

A Full Plans application must be supported by detailed plans and is thoroughly checked by the local authority. If your plans comply you will be issued with an approval notice. With a Building Notice application less detailed plans are required but no approval notice is given and you can be asked to submit more detailed plans and calculations at a later date.

What is planning permission?
To protect the environment of our cities, towns and countryside, a detailed series of regulations have been drawn up. Planned alterations to your property must comply with these regulations if you are not to fall foul of the law. If you build or alter without planning permission, you can be forced to put things right at a later date. This can of course be costly, time consuming and troublesome, even including pulling down an office extension for instance!

Do you need planning permission?
All planning applications are examined by the local authorities, who treat each on its individual merits. As you might expect there are many grey areas, where it is difficult to decide if you need consent or not.

In addition to standard planning regulations, special types of planning approval are needed when the following are involved:

- listed buildings
- conservation sites
- areas of outstanding natural beauty
- a national park
- protected trees

You should be able to work out if you need planning permission by answering the following questions:

1. Will the main use of your house still be as a family home?

   Yes ☐   No ☐

   If you are not using more than one room then there should be no problems. However, should your business grow so that you take over more and more of the house then you may require planning consent. You may also run into problems with your mortgage company.

2. Will you be employing more than one person on a regular basis?

   Yes ☐   No ☐

   As soon as others come into your house to work then theoretically you may need planning permission. In the main commonsense should apply. If you employ only one or two others they should cause little nuisance to others.

3. Will your work generate calls from suppliers and customers to your house?

   Yes ☐   No ☐

   If lorries block the street as they unload to your house, you are asking for trouble. The same can be said if customers or clients are continually ringing your doorbell and taking up all the parking spaces in the street.

4. Will you need to promote your business with external advertising or a nameplate?

   Yes ☐   No ☐

   If you need to advertise your presence with a sign, then you are almost certain to need planning permission. However, those under 0.3 square metres on the front of your property are allowable. Larger ones need consent.

5. Will your business involve noise, fumes or involve anti-social hours?

   Yes ☐   No ☐

   If your business is going to produce much noise, fumes and/or involve anti-social hours then sooner or later you are going to receive complaints from the neighbours and the interest of the planning authorities, who have the right to order you to stop.

6. Will you need to park a trade vehicle on your premises?

   Yes ☐   No ☐

Trade or delivery vehicles parked up at your house may require you to have planning permission.

If you have answered 'Yes' to a few of these questions then your business is perhaps not ideal for homeworking and you may be better off looking for premises elsewhere.

Should you go ahead regardless, you might of course get away without having planning permission for a few months, perhaps even a year, but the chances are that you will eventually be caught.

When you are, the planning authorities can order you to stop trading from home. This will not only affect your trade, but involve you in expense and inconvenience as you will have to find new premises, change all of your stationery and telephone number and inform your clients and suppliers through advertising and letters that you are moving. A young business can do without such disruption.

Should you have any doubts about your business, check with the local planning authorities. If you feel that you are operating in a grey area, it may be worth discussing your situation with a planning consultant rather than informing the local authorities and involving them unnecessarily.

What if I want to build an office extension?

You will need to apply for planning permission for an office extension if:

- you want to build an extension that is nearer the highway (most public roads and some footpaths) than the nearest part of the 'original house' (the house as it was built or as it's been since 1st July 1948).

- over half of the land area around the house is to be covered by extensions or other buildings.

- if you add an office extension that adds over 10% (or over fifty cubic metres) to the volume of your original house if your house is a terrace or in a Conservation Area, National Park, an Area of Outstanding Natural Beauty or the Norfolk Broads.

- if you add an office extension that adds over 15% (or over seventy cubic metres) to the volume of your original house if your house is outside these areas.

How to apply for planning permission

If you think that you need planning permission for your intended alterations then contact your local planning department; they are part of the local council. Explain what you hope to do and ask for their advice. They will give you an application form if they think your plans may require planning permission. Ask them if they foresee any potential problems which you could avoid by altering your proposals.

There are two types of application you can make. A **Full Application** is required when you know exactly what you intend to do and have detailed drawings to support your application. However, you can submit an **Outline Application** if you simply want to see what the council thinks of your building intentions before you commission or produce detailed drawings. You will still have to submit detailed drawings at a later stage.

- Several copies of the application form may need to be sent to the planning department, along with a fee, a plan of the site and copy of the drawings which show the work you intend to carry out. The council will tell you which drawings these should be.

What happens next?

The receipt of your application will be acknowledged within a few days. The application will then be placed on the **Planning Register** at the local council offices where it can be inspected by members of the general public. At this stage your neighbours may be notified and highway authorities and parish councils consulted.

People can object to your plans, and copies of their objections may be obtained from the council offices. You will probably help your cause if you tell your neighbours of any alterations that will affect them by spoiling their view or taking their light.

A report may be prepared for the planning committee by the planning department, though a senior planning officer may be given the job of deciding the merits of your application.

Your application should be decided within eight weeks. If it cannot be, then the planning authorities should ask you if they extend the time limit.

Your planning application will be decided on whether it will essentially affect the local area adversely, or should be approved if certain conditions are met. The council must give its reasons for refusing permission or imposing conditions.

What if planning permission is refused?

You can submit another planning application at no cost within twelve months of the first application. Ask the planning authorities if making changes to your plans would make them more acceptable.

How to complete a planning application

For most homeworkers completing a planning application is a simple matter. A typical example is shown in Figure 1, with the homeworker seeking to build an extension which will serve as an office.

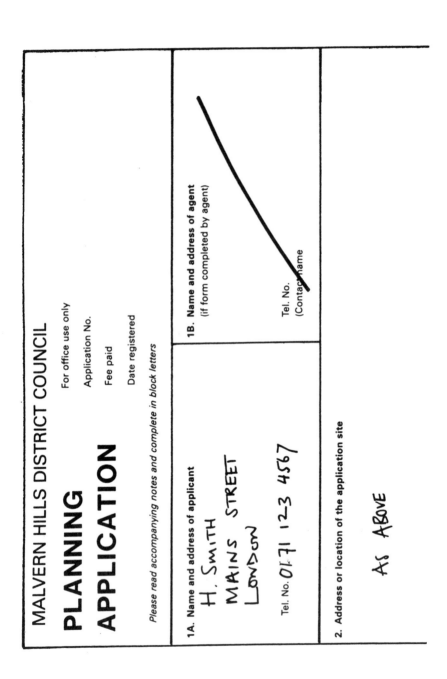

Fig. 1. A planning application form.

3. Brief description of proposed development *EXTENSION TO THE REAR OF THE ABOVE PROPERTY. THE EXTENSION WILL MEASURE 5m x 5m x 3m. IT WILL BE MADE FROM BRICK WITH A ROOF OF SLATE. IT WILL SERVE AS A STUDY/FOURTH BEDROOM*

Site Area _____ (Hectares)

4. Type of application (Please tick one box)
- (a) This is a full application for a change of use only and does not involve any building works at present ☐
- (b) This is a full application for change of use and/or new building works ☑
- (c) This is an outline application ☐ (Answer Question 5)
- (d) This is an application for the approval of matters reserved under a previous permission ☐ (Answer Question 6)
- (e) This is an application for removal or modification of a condition ☐
- (f) This is an application for the renewal of a temporary permission (give No. _____) ☐

5. Outline application (If you ticked (c) in Question 4, please tick one or more boxes)
The following matters are reserved for future consideration
Siting ☐ Design ☐ Details of Access ☐ Landscape Proposals ☐ Materials ☐

6. Approval of reserved matters (If you ticked (d) in Question 4, please complete)
- (a) Please state Reference Number of previous outline permission
- (b) Please state which reserved matters are dealt with in this application

(Please tick one or more boxes)
Siting ☐ Design ☐ Details of Access ☐ Landscape Proposals ☐ Materials ☐

P.1. (Rev 90).

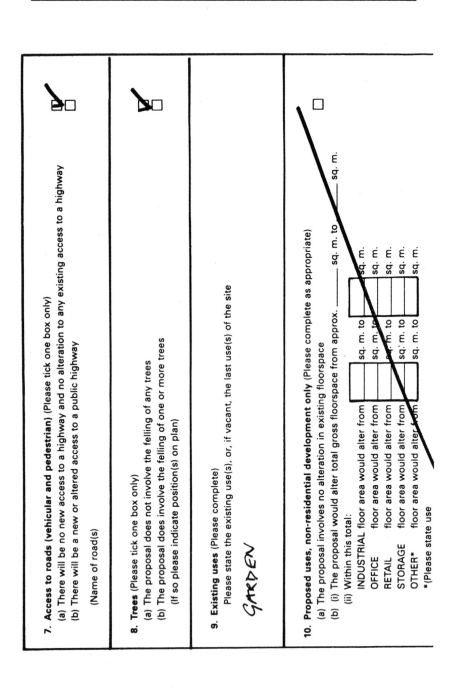

7. Access to roads (vehicular and pedestrian) (Please tick one box only)

(a) There will be no new access to a highway and no alteration to any existing access to a highway ☑

(b) There will be a new or altered access to a public highway ☐

(Name of road(s)

8. Trees (Please tick one box only)

(a) The proposal does not involve the felling of any trees ☑

(b) The proposal does involve the felling of one or more trees ☐

(If so please indicate position(s) on plan)

9. Existing uses (Please complete)

Please state the existing use(s), or, if vacant, the last use(s) of the site

GARDEN

10. Proposed uses, non-residential development only (Please complete as appropriate) ☐

(a) The proposal involves no alteration in existing floorspace

(b) (i) The proposal would alter total gross floorspace from approx. _____ sq. m. to _____ sq. m.

(ii) Within this total:

INDUSTRIAL floor area would alter from	☐ sq. m. to	☐ sq. m.
OFFICE floor area would alter from	☐ sq. m. to	☐ sq. m.
RETAIL floor area would alter from	☐ sq. m. to	☐ sq. m.
STORAGE floor area would alter from	☐ sq. m. to	☐ sq. m.
OTHER* floor area would alter from	☐ sq. m. to	☐ sq. m.

*(Please state use

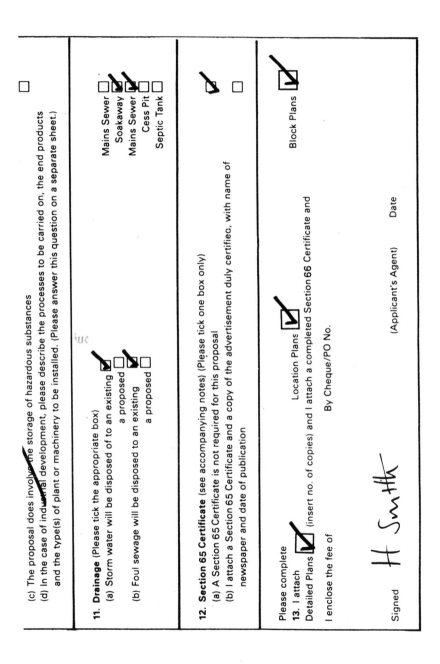

(c) The proposal does involve the storage of hazardous substances ☐

(d) In the case of industrial development, please describe the processes to be carried on, the end products and the type(s) of plant or machinery to be installed. (Please answer this question on a separate sheet.)

11. Drainage (Please tick the appropriate box)

(a) Storm water will be disposed of to an existing / a proposed ☐

(b) Foul sewage will be disposed to an existing / a proposed ☐

Mains Sewer ☐
Soakaway ☑
Mains Sewer ☑
Cess Pit ☐
Septic Tank ☐

12. Section 65 Certificate (see accompanying notes) (Please tick one box only)

(a) A Section 65 Certificate is not required for this proposal ☑

(b) I attach a Section 65 Certificate and a copy of the advertisement duly certified, with name of newspaper and date of publication ☐

Please complete

13. I attach   Location Plans ☑   Block Plans ☑
Detailed Plans ☑ (insert no. of copies) and I attach a completed Section 66 Certificate and

I enclose the fee of   By Cheque/PO No.

Signed H Smith   (Applicant's Agent)   Date

1A.   Simply fill in your name, address and telephone number. You will not need to fill in 1B unless someone is working on your behalf, such as an architect.

2.   This will be the address of your home.

3.   The basic details of any extension, its size, location and general appearance are sufficient here. Describing the extension as an office could cause tax problems if it is perceived you are using part of your home exclusively for commercial or business purposes. It is perhaps better described as a study or fourth or fifth bedroom.

        If you are not extending your house, but intend to alter the character and use of your building so that it does not remain essentially the same, then you should outline your plans here. A change in character might occur if your business will result in a marked rise in the amount of traffic or number of people calling on you, or if your business will disturb neighbours, or if your business will generate activities that are unusual in residential areas. There is no real need to include the area of your garden or grounds.

4a.   Tick this box if you want to change the use of the building, for instance to turn your house into a shop, but are not yet ready to undertake building work. (Generally homeworkers will not be seeking to change the use of their home.) A full application must include detailed plans of the building work.

4b.   Most homeworkers will tick this box, as this section deals with new building works (the planned extension).

4c.   An outline application allows you to find out whether permission will be given in principle without having to submit detailed and expensive drawings. Even if your outline application is accepted you will still have to submit detailed plans at a later date if you make a full permission.

4d, e, f. These sections are relevant only if you have applied for planning permission previously.

5 & 6. If you apply (or have applied) for outline permission you may have no detailed thoughts on aspects of your plan, such as material you will use or the exact design. This section allows you to finalise details at a later date.

7.   This should affect few homeworkers.

8.   If you are not intending to fell trees to build an office extension or alter access, tick the first box.

9.   'Garden' or 'amenity area to house' is generally sufficient to describe the existing use of the site.

10.   Not relevant for those working from home.

11a.   Provision must be made to take away the water that flows off the roof of an extension. In town it is usual to send rainwater via the downpipe into an *existing* Mains Sewer (tick the relevant boxes). Where this is not possible the water will be sent to a *proposed* Soakaway (tick the relevant boxes).

11b.   Rather than leave this section blank, it is best to indicate that Foul sewage will be disposed off to an existing system, even if your extension is not to have a lavatory.

12a.   A completed section 65 Certificate, obtainable from your local planning authority, is required only if you are applying for planning permission on land that does not belong to you. Unlikely in the case of the homeworker.

13.   Detailed plans are those that show the nature, extent and character of the proposed building work or changes.

        Location plans should show the boundary of your property and local surrounds – 1/2500th scale is generally acceptable.

        Block plans show the position of your property, the proposed extension and a few neighbouring properties and features in greater detail and size than on location plans.

CHECKING YOUR HOUSE DEEDS

Many houses, and nearly all residential flats, contain conditions in their deeds that limit and restrict business activities.

Some deeds carry a total ban which could read something like 'not to carry on upon the premises any trade, business or profession whatsoever,' while others merely prohibit certain businesses such as 'not to sell upon the premises any beers, wines or spirituous liquors'.

If the covenant says that you cannot carry on an 'obnoxious' or 'objectionable' business then you should have no problems running an accountancy practice, or computer programming business. And though your deeds may prohibit the carrying on of a 'trade or business', this has been held not to stop you carrying on a 'learned profession'.

Even though they may be many years old, such restrictive covenants remain in force even though you may have received planning permission for your business venture.

If you break the covenant then anyone who receives benefit from the restrictive covenant, such as your next door neighbour, could apply to the court for an injunction to stop you working from home.

Would-be home entrepreneurs can apply to the court to have restrictive covenants discharged. Though the best course of action is to seek professional help and advice from your solicitor, answering the following questions should give you a good idea of whether a covenant will prevent you using your house or flat for your work.

Checklist

1. Do the deeds specifically prohibit the use of your home for your particular business?

   Yes ☐   No ☐

2. If you breach the covenant will this have such a detrimental effect on your neighbours that they will want to stop you doing business?

   Yes ☐   No ☐

3. The covenant may have lapsed if the persons entitled to its benefit, for instance the neighbours, have allowed the owner to carry on the business for a long time without trying to stop him or her. Has this happened?

   Yes ☐   No ☐

4. Times change and if the nature of the district has considerably altered, then the covenant may not be relevant. Is this the case?

   Yes ☐   No ☐

CHECKING ANY MORTGAGE RESTRICTIONS

Out of courtesy you should let your mortgage company know you intend to work from home. Most lenders will raise no objections. However, if your work raises the likelihood of damage to the house, say if you are a painter and decorator storing inflammable paints, there may be problems over your insurance cover. This of course won't be a problem for most homeworkers who want to set up an office just to handle paperwork and generate sales.

Also, if a large part of the house, rather than just one room, is to be used for work, then a mortgage company may consider that their money, originally loaned for residential purposes, has been transformed into a commercial loan. As commercial interest rates are generally higher than residential, you are getting a good deal and they are losing out.

If you make or intend to make extensive alterations to your house then there is the possibility that you may be reducing the value of your house which could considerably devalue your house. Then the mortgage company may not be able to get their money back if they had to sell the house.

HOMEWORKING AND YOUR TENANCY AGREEMENT

Again this depends on your business. But if you do not require planning permission then you should have few problems if you are a local authority tenant. However, those who are the tenants of private landlords may not be so fortunate. Always check before beginning business. If you have difficulties seek advice from a solicitor or your local Citizens Advice Bureau.

GETTING INSURANCE

Working from home may invalidate the normal comprehensive householder policy which otherwise applies. If you equip your home with the latest in office equipment or electronic machinery then it is sensible to ensure that you are adequately insured. Often your general household insurance may go some way to covering your work equipment, but not all of it.

You should remember that many policies have a single item limit, say £1,000 or £1,500—a computer can cost much more than that, so you will be out of pocket if you have to replace it.

Insurance companies vary in their attitudes. Some may take the view that if you bring people, either staff or clients, into your house then the risk of theft increases, and you may have to pay an additional premium. Others may consider that if someone is at home all day then there is less chance of the house being burgled.

You may be able to negotiate a reduction in the premium if you can show that your home is sufficiently protected and secure. Fortunately many house break-ins are committed by opportunist thieves who are deterred by a few simple and low-cost precautions that make life difficult for them and increase the chances of them being caught.

However, if a burglar really wants to get into your home then he will, but there is no point in making it easy for him and adding a wealth of high-tech and valuable equipment to his haul. Window locks, well lit alleyways, deadlocks on doors, joining the Neighbourhood Watch and even fitting an alarm system can all discourage the casual thief.

All you can do is seek advice from a broker, but be prepared to pay a higher premium to cover office equipment. After all an insurance company could be involved in a substantial payment, far greater than the average domestic claim, should you be burgled and your fax, computer and photocopier stolen.

If you think that the additional premium is unreasonable then shop around for a better deal. However, beware of penny pinching, the cheapest deal is not always the best. Paying a few more pounds to a reputable company that pays up quickly is better than having to haggle with another less accommodating company at a later date. The last thing you want is a disputed insurance claim when you need to get on with your business.

Case history 1 – Janet has a narrow escape

When she began to homework, Janet, an accountant, made sure that her insurance covered all of her large pieces of office equipment: computer, printer, fax and photocopier. (She had noted down their serial numbers and marked each item with her postcode using an 'invisible' marker pen.) As a further protection she had strong security locks fitted to all of her windows and doors and joined the Neighbourhood Watch scheme. Her husband thought that this was all a bit too much, especially when Janet was at home most of the time.

Then one day, when Janet was at a meeting with clients, the house was broken into—or at least almost. Not only had the window locks defeated the thief, but he had spent so long trying to get in that a neighbour had seen him and telephoned the police.

Case history 2 – Dennis is burgled

Dennis had a lot of high-tech equipment in his office, but he lived in a rural area where there was very little crime, so he was lax about his insurance and house security.

When there was a sudden spate of burglaries in the area Dennis told himself he ought to take out some more insurance cover, but never quite got around to it before the thieves broke in. They took all of his office equipment, plus his television and video—about £6,000 in all.

Unfortunately for Dennis, he was only covered for £1,800! To replace the lost equipment took nearly all of Dennis's savings. The theft ruined his business plan for the year and almost put him out of business.

How to insure yourself and your income

If you work from your home then you are reliant on your own efforts to bring in work. If you cannot work then you do not earn and illness and accidents can happen to anyone. Having to take a few days off with the flu would probably be more annoying than uncomfortable, but imagine if you had a car crash that laid you up for a couple of weeks, a month, six months! Could you survive on your savings?

There are, however, insurance schemes that protect your income should you fall ill or become disabled. Not unexpectedly they do not cover you simply because you cannot find work. However, not all occupations are covered by such schemes, either because they are dangerous or too erratic. Fortunately most homeworkers will be covered, even falling into a low-risk category, so premiums are minimal. The monthly premium is in part dependent on how much you need to receive each month, but the relatively small expenditure is well worth the protection they give.

For the future you should also begin a pension plan as soon as possible. This will supplement the small low pensions provided by the state. If your income is variable then you should choose one that has a high degree of flexibility and that allows you to vary contributions or even temporarily put off paying them altogether. Pension premiums are tax deductible.

Depending on your line of business it may be wise to take out **professional indemnity insurance**. This gives you some protection should the advice you give lead to financial or legal problems for others through bad administration or manufacture. Your insurance broker will be able to advise. The premiums will depend on the nature of your business and how much cover you want to provide.

In addition, should you start employing others (even if they are a relative) then you require **employer's liability insurance**. This will cover you should your employee be injured or become sick whilst working for you.

PAYING TAX AS A HOMEWORKER

Even though you may work from home it may not mean that you are self-employed and eligible for their tax advantages. Particularly for teleworkers, who primarily work for one employer, this can be something of a grey area as they are often still regarded as being employees.

Are you self-employed or not?
In recent years, the Inland Revenue have been slowly working through a whole range of professions and even though freelancers may have worked for twenty or thirty different employers during the year, it is no guarantee that you will be regarded as self-employed.

Before you begin working from home you should notify the Inland Revenue telling them that you are becoming self-employed or are forming a company. Your accountant will be able to advise on the way to keep your books.

Checking your status
Your answers to the following questions should give a good indication of whether you are self-employed or an employee.

1. Do you work for more than one client?

      Yes ☐   No ☐

If you have essentially just one work source then the taxman will probably regard you as being an employee. Of course he will consider the length of time that you have had only this one supplier of work.

2. Are you supplied with equipment by someone else?

   Yes ☐   No ☐

   If you are then you will probably be regarded as an employee.

3. Are you largely able to decide how you will work?

   Yes ☐   No ☐

   If someone else can tell you largely what to do, when to do it, where and how, then you are likely to be regarded as an employee.

4. Do you keep your own accounts and business records?

   Yes ☐   No ☐

   If you do then you are most likely in business for yourself and not an employee.

Is Capital Gains Tax a problem?

Generally there are not too many extra problems regarding tax and working from home. The main tax that could affect home-based workers is Capital Gains Tax. If part of your property is given over exclusively to business, that is if it has been converted into an office and cannot be used as living space, then there could be a Capital Gains Tax liability.

Some accountants now suggest that their clients claim a percentage of their total mortgage interest payments as work expenditure against tax. There is some debate however, on whether this makes you eligible for business rates! The sensible thing is to take advice from your accountant.

PAYING NATIONAL INSURANCE CONTRIBUTIONS

If you become self-employed then you become responsible for your own National Insurance Contributions. These are of two types. The first are regular Class 2 payments, which you can pay by direct debit each month. However, you are also liable for Class 4 contributions which are related to the level of your profits. There are paid at the same time as your tax bill. These National Insurance Contributions do not give the same benefits as they do for an employee. For instance, you cannot claim Unemployment Benefit.

CLAIMING SICKNESS BENEFIT

Many individuals who work for themselves from home, do not realise that they can claim sickness benefit should they fall ill. Eligibility for benefit is based on your recent earnings and you must be prepared to show evidence in the form of accounts or tax statements. Any claim must be made at the time you are ill. If you don't do this then you are not eligible for any benefit. If you need to claim the benefit then you must complete the self certification form (SC1) from your local social security office. After a week of illness you will need to obtain a sickness certificate from your doctor to claim the benefit. You can claim benefit as long as a doctor certifies that you are sick.

VAT AND THE HOMEWORKER

With Value Added Tax (VAT) you collect tax on behalf of the Government which allows you to deduct the VAT on supplies and services that you have paid in the course of your business. Effectively for many items you are paying 17½% less for an item than you would if you were not registered for VAT. However, on the other side, you must increase your prices by a similar amount.

The money that you collect in VAT can be kept for about three months, so improving the finances of your company for a limited time and earning you interest.

Every business can register for VAT, though not all of them need to. However, you must register for VAT if your annual gross turnover exceeds £46,000.

Registering for VAT will involve you in more paperwork which must be completed each quarter. Some businesses that have been VAT registered for more than a year and have a turnover of less than £300,000 can apply for annual VAT accounting.

Under normal VAT arrangements you must pay the VAT you owe, even if you have not received that money from your customers. This can generate a bad cash flow if someone is late in paying you. With the annual scheme you only pay the difference between the amount of VAT you have received and the amount of VAT you have paid out.

Homeworkers could face a VAT charge on the light and heating of their office if they claim part of it as a business expense. Since July 1990, the standard rate of VAT has been applied to electricity, gas, oil and solid fuels. This particular tax is unlikely to bother you unless you claim that at least 40% of your total fuel bill is for business use. Your accountant will be able to give further information and advice on all VAT matters.

COUNCIL TAX

Self-employed homeworkers cannot offset part of their council tax against income tax, as a legitimate business expense, which could be done with the old rating system.

HEALTH AND SAFETY REGULATIONS

The Health and Safety Act covers everyone who is at work, which includes anyone who works from home. Theoretically therefore you are obliged to abide by its regulations and stipulations. However, since a Health and Safety inspector could only enter your home with your permission, in effect you can do what you like at home.

The European Union (EU) is becoming increasingly involved with all aspects of our lives and this is one of them. In particular, EU Council Directive (90/270 EEC) lays down minimum safety and health requirements for computer screens or VDUs. This requires employers to evaluate the risk to their staff from computer equipment, software and the office environment. The directive expects employers to keep abreast of changes in technology and scientific research. It came into force in 1993.

However, if you work from home, but with someone else supplying your equipment, such as a computer, then that equipment should be of the same standard as equipment in a factory or office where Health and Safety regulations do apply. Should you start employing part or full-time staff, who work from your house, then your home immediately ceases to be a 'home' and becomes 'a place of work' where Health and Safety regulations do apply.

THE DATA PROTECTION ACT

Introduced in 1987, the Data Protection Act is a complicated piece of legislation that has far reaching implications. It was introduced to curb abuses of powerful computer systems capable of storing and exploiting the information they held on people.

For homeworkers the Data Protection Act becomes relevant when they keep information, no matter how little, on computer about any living person. If you do this, or intend to, then you must register under the Data Protection Act. There are a few exceptions to the Act which cover only the simplest of tasks, such as calculating pay and pensions of staff, keeping accounts, distributing articles or mailing lists, or preparing the text of documents.

However, if you start using your accounts records as a mailing list, or have a mailing which contains more information that just a name, address and telephone number then you are obliged to register.

Once you are registered then individuals can ask to see any computerised information that you hold on them and if the information is incorrect have it altered or sometimes deleted. If incorrect information has damaged them, then they can also claim compensation against you.

3
Designing Your Office

SPOKEN FROM EXPERIENCE

'Few DIY tasks are more satisfying than creating a room, or a section of a room, which is a pleasure to work in.' Terence Conran, designer.
'Space. The final frontier.' Captain James T. Kirk, *Starship Enterprise.*

WHY YOU NEED AN OFFICE

It is possible to work from home and not have an office, but this is very far from ideal and will seriously hinder your productivity. But for the serious homeworker, a dedicated home office really is an essential. No matter how small that office is, you should make every effort to create a working space that is solely yours. There are very good reasons for this:

- A dedicated home office gives you a secure place from which to work. This is your space and within reason you will be able to do with it what you want.

- When you work from your own office, you minimise the number of interruptions to which you can fall prey. You will never work effectively if you have to use a living room in which people are moving about, or the television is on.

- In any business, papers quickly proliferate and they must have a home. So too must your computer, filing cabinets, telephone, fax machine, stationery and much else. A dedicated home office allows you to organise your material and keep it to hand.

If you have to take out and then clear away all of your equipment and papers every day, you waste time and add extra tiredness and irritation to your working day. In your own office you can start a project and leave papers arranged in the way you want them without having to tidy up when it is time for dinner, or if visitors unexpectedly arrive.

STARTING YOUR DESIGN

Home offices are as different as the people who work in them. Within reason, you should take as much care as you can in designing, laying out and equipping your office as possible to ensure that it suits you—the person who will work in it.

Not only must a home office create an environment in which you can work productively, but it must also have a comfortable atmosphere. After all who wants to spend fifty or sixty hours each week working in a place they find depressing?

Generally, your scope for developing the home office *you* want will be limited by the size of your house and the number of people living in it and their reactions to you working from home.

Offices come in all shapes and sizes. Very often the homeworker is relegated to the second smallest room in the house, usually the tiniest, coldest or most uncomfortable of spare bedrooms.

Sometimes it is possible to swap with someone in the family who has a more suitable room, but win their co-operation first. Evicting a teenage son or daughter from their larger room is to court a furious adolescent rebellion.

How much space do you need?

Generally a room that is roughly ten to twelve feet long and six to eight feet wide is a good office size. The smaller the room available to you, the more you must use your imagination and design skills to overcome the problems that lack of space creates, such as the amount of equipment, furniture and shelving that you can have. Home offices have been created from the sloping space beneath the stairs!

The smaller your office the greater need to keep it unfussy and not full of bits and pieces that have nothing to do with work. Lots of ornaments and frills around will make your office harder to clean and occupy space which could be otherwise used.

An upstairs office or a downstairs one?

For most purposes there is little difference in being upstairs or down, but one word of warning. If your office is upstairs several four-drawer filing cabinets full of paper are a terrific weight. This can put an extraordinary stress on an unsound floor.

To avoid a highly unpleasant and expensive accident, relegate the filing cabinets containing less regularly used papers to the garage or a downstairs room and make do with just a couple of two-drawer cabinets up in your office. If the floor is particularly suspect then position the cabinets in different parts of the room, preferably above a sound joist.

Creating extra space

Most homeworkers will at some time or another need more space in their office. Some minor alterations and adjustments can give the extra area that you need.

- Stud partition walls are easily removed. Without too much difficulty you might be able to knock a boxroom and bedroom together. In the same way, unwanted built-in wardrobes can be opened up. Before you remove any wall, even a stud partition wall, make sure it is not a load bearing one. Check if the wall runs in the same direction as the joists (at right angles to the floorboards). If it does then it is unlikely to be load bearing and can be knocked down without affecting the structure of the house. Consult a builder or architect if you are unsure.

- Try removing any doors you don't need, such as those separating one section of the room from another. This not only makes you feel as though you have more space, but means you can move cabinets and bookshelves further along walls where doors would normally open. Swapping hinged doors for sliding or folding ones creates the same effect.

- Radiators may be in the wrong position for your purposes. Sometimes they can be moved at relatively low cost to free up additional space.

- False ceilings reduce the height of rooms in some houses, especially Victorian ones. Remove the ceilings and you may reveal another two feet of space which can be used for extra shelving, or to give the feeling of greater 'airiness' in your office. A moveable or sliding ladder could be used to reach this high storage area.

- Enlarging windows lets extra light into your office, making it look larger and more attractive to work in. However, this does reduce wall space for shelves. Improved lighting may be a better answer.

HOW TO DECORATE YOUR OFFICE

Do not despair if you are generally stumped by colour schemes and interior decor. The main principle behind decorating a home office is 'keep it simple'. All that you are trying to do is create a light, pleasant and comfortable working environment, which you won't mind being in for many hours a day.

Walls and ceilings

Wherever possible, simply coat office walls and ceiling with a good quality paint. This has the advantages of being cheap and easy to do, which can't be said about wallpapering.

Matt paint is best; glossy finishes produce distracting reflections that all too soon become annoying and irritate the eyes.

Choose colours with which you feel comfortable, but try to use a light colour such as white, magnolia or cream, rather than dark ones. This makes your office look roomier and these colours match with most others.

Colours are said to affect our moods and emotions: yellow being 'sunny'; blue, cool and calming; while red is said to stimulate. Don't be too daring. Being stimulated or 'brightened' all day long can become just a little too much.

If you do wallpaper, avoid bold images or patterns as these, like strong paint colours, become tiresome very quickly, especially in a small room.

Floor coverings

If it is not already, carpet the room. This is not only more comfortable underfoot than tiles or linoleum, but cuts down on noise, particularly important if you work from an upstairs room. People in the living room won't want to hear the sounds of you, your printer and fax machine when they are watching 'Coronation Street'! Don't floor with shiny tiles as they produce unwanted glare.

Of course these are only general rules and everyone has their own thoughts on what works best for them. Some people for instance feel far happier in an almost claustrophobic environment. Their offices are painted in dark colours which 'draw in' the walls to give a womb-like feel. This they believe concentrates the mind on the task in hand.

WORKING IN THE RIGHT LIGHT

From the gloom of early morning, through the brightness of midday to the pitch-black of night, which in mid-winter begins at five, you will spend long hours in your office.

Straining your eyes in semi-darkness through lack of good lighting will quickly tire them and make you less productive. When you are in your office, you have to be able to see properly and to do that you need good, adequate natural and electric lighting.

Most of us feel more confident when we stand in the sun rather than in gloom. An office that is filled with light can be psychologically uplifting, for example if you have to make a difficult telephone call.

Where to put your desk

Ideally position your desk at right angles to the window. Here you achieve the most even spread of light falling onto your work. If you sit with your back to the window you either cast a dark shadow onto your work, or have it 'floodlit' by the midday sun forcing its way over your shoulder.

And if your desk faces the window, not only will your eyes continually have to adjust from outside brightness to the relative gloom of indoors, but you will also be able to see the world and his wife go by. Another source of distraction that you can well do without. If you want to window gaze, then make it a five minute treat. A reward to yourself after a good session of work.

For those who spend a lot of time at the computer, the right lighting is particularly important. Too much sun, or electric light shining on the screen creates bad reflections that cause eye-strain. This is one of the prime causes of headaches and eye-strain at the 'computer face'.

Whenever possible work at the computer in a slightly darkened room. This minimises the changes your eyes must make when moving from the computer screen to the brighter background of your office.

Blinds are better than curtains at regulating the flow of light into your office. They allow you to darken the room on bright summer days and let in more light on dark winter ones.

Try to create an open space beyond the desk so that your eyes can focus on more distant objects from time to time. After a lot of close work, switching your gaze into open space relaxes your eyes.

What type of lights should you have?

Most standard domestic rooms are equipped with a pendant fitting that really only lights the centre of the room, shrouding corners in gloom and casting shadows across any desk set near a wall.

If this is the case, move the light to an area that really needs illumination, such as around shelving or the fax machine. The neatest way of doing this is to pull electric cable through the roof space above and reposition the light where you want it. If you are not DIY-minded then leave this to an electrician.

A simpler, though less attractive way of achieving the same effect is to run a longer length of electric cord from the central pendant. This is hung over a hook, screwed into the ceiling above the area you want lit.

Just as with dim light, working when it is too bright is also very tiring. For more accurate control of your environment, fit a dimmer switch so that you can accurately regulate light levels, but fit 100 watt bulbs so that you have brightness when you want or need it.

Standard incandescent lighting is softer and less harsh than fluorescent lighting. This can hum noisily, which is particularly irritating in a small space, and can also cause headaches with its flickering. If you do intend to work under fluorescent light try not to position your desk so that you look at them end on.

Whatever main lighting you choose, this should be supplemented by a light at your desk. This removes the hard shadows produced by a single light source and concentrates the mind wonderfully on just the job in hand.

Desk lights can either be freestanding, or clipped to the side of the desk. Choose a light that can be angled, lowered and raised easily so as not to throw any glare onto a computer screen. Make sure that the light will stay in its new position, lamps that suddenly droop are an aggravation.

PLANNING THE LAYOUT

If possible, base your office layout on a L-shape. The 'bottom' of the L should be your desk with the rest of the equipment wrapping around to the right. If you are left-handed then the L's long arm should be to the right.

Try to set up the items that you most frequently use in the form of a triangle. For example, one point of the triangle could be the computer, another the filing cabinet that holds your day-to-day papers, and the third the open worktop at right angles to your main work table.

By organising space in this way you keep your movements to a minimum. Should there be five or six items that you move regularly between each day then lay out your office in a semi-circle. If your chair swivels, then for most of the day you will be able to reach everything you need without even having to stand up.

Don't arrange your work space in a straight line. To shift between computer, desktop, fax machine and filing cabinets you will have to make many more movements, each of them eating into valuable work time.

Ensure that at least some shelves are near your desk. Here frequently consulted books such as trade manuals, dictionaries, factfinders and telephone directories should be kept.

It is worth creating a 'to go' area near the door. This could be part of a desk or a small table on which outgoing mail, library books and other items destined for the outside world, are kept. Putting them here means that you are less likely to forget them and they remain out of the way whilst you carry on with the rest of your office work.

If you want to use your office as a meeting place for clients or suppliers, then create a more comfortable area where you can sit away from desktops and computers. Most people however will lack the space to do this.

Figure 2 shows the layout for a compact home office. All of the important equipment can be reached with a quarter to half turn from the chair. Light from the window falls at 90 degrees to the computer, keeping glare off the screen. The computer table is deep enough for the screen to be far enough away to prevent eye-strain. The narrower desk at right

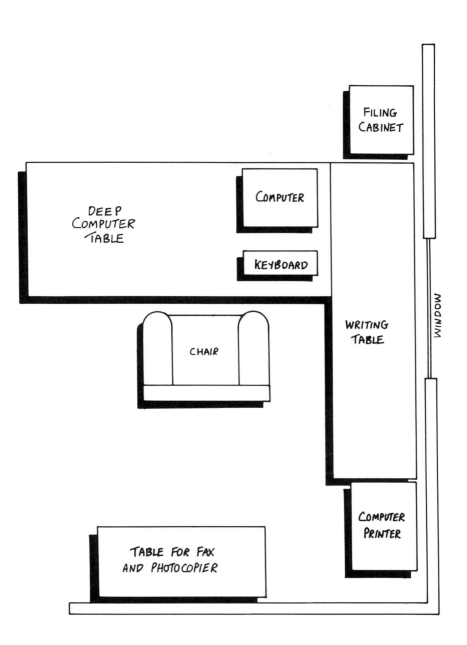

Fig. 2. Layout for a compact home office.

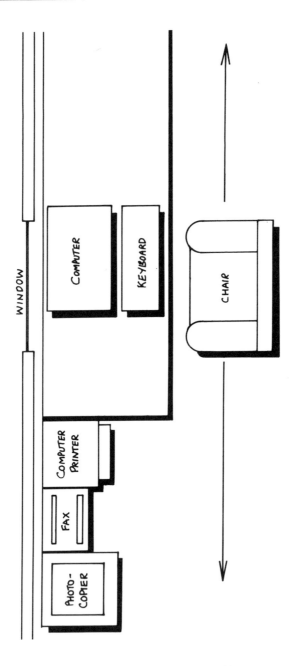

Fig. 3. The kind of layout to avoid.

angles to the computer table is used for written work.

A poor layout is shown in Figure 3. By positioning everything in a straight line, you can only reach certain items by moving your chair or getting up out of it. If filing cabinets and bookshelves were also incorporated into this straight line layout, the situation would become even worse. The computer is also in the wrong place. Sun shining through the window would dazzle the eyes, and just to make matters worse, the table is too narrow so that you would have to sit 'on top' of the computer. A certain recipe for eye-strain.

HOW TO DESIGN YOUR HOME OFFICE

Power and heat
The important thing to remember about electrical sockets is that you can't have too many of them. In a well equipped home office the computer, printer, answer machine, fax, photocopier, modem and maybe clock radio would each require a socket, a total of at least seven electric points.

Heating your office
You must make sure that your office is adequately heated. You will not do good work if by turns you are either shivering to death or sweltering in a heat wave.

If your office is a cold one you will have to have some form of supplementary heating, either electric or gas. Good double glazing and insulation in the roof space will also do their bit in keeping you warm. Fitting blinds can help reduce the heat in summer. Beware of portable fans, unless you have a breeze coming into the room all they do is circulate warm air, and even add to the temperature through their motor.

Around sixty-five to seventy degrees Fahrenheit (twenty-two to twenty-four degrees Centigrade) is a good temperature level to aim for. Stray too much from this and you will either slow down with the cold or begin to wilt in the heat.

Your changing office
Though it is important to create a good working environment for yourself, a home office is only a means to an end, not an end in itself. Do not try to be a perfectionist at the beginning as your office will evolve with your needs. You want to establish your office as quickly as possible, not win design awards.

Spending a lot of money on creating your office at an early stage can be money wasted, if you find that after a few weeks the layout doesn't work for you. So when starting to work from home, concentrate your finances on office equipment rather than office design.

Complete your basic decoration, add more electric sockets if needed and make sure that your lighting is adequate. These things will be more difficult to alter once furniture is in place. Set a time limit for all of this. Unless you are really going to town on a tailor-made work-room, then you should be able to complete your office in a week to ten days.

OTHER OPTIONS

The purpose-built office

Some companies offer to design and build a fitted home office that suits your needs and blends into the home. For those with the money, this may be an option. But remember you only have one chance at getting the design right. Should your needs change it is more difficult and expensive to include new equipment or work space. You could make a costly mistake, so why try and impress someone with an elegant, but expensive custom-built office when few others are going to see it?

If that is what you want to do, then at least start designing and working in your office for six months to a year so that at least you understand your needs.

Using someone else's home

If you cannot find enough space in your own house for an office, try going to someone else's. Does a nearby neighbour have a spare room that you might be able to rent or loan?

It is not the best solution, but if you both feel comfortable with the situation it is worth exploring. If you travel this route, decide carefully and clearly at the beginning what ground rules are going to hold between you and your neighbour.

You need to answer such questions as: how many, if any, structural alterations can you make? Will you be allowed to decorate? When will you be allowed to use the office, early in the morning or late at night? Will you be given a key to the house? What facilities in the house will you be allowed to use? Will you pay rent, if so how much?

Obviously the better the relationship you have with your 'landlords' the more flexibility you have.

The tabletop office

If you cannot find space for an office either at home or nearby, then you will have to use a desk or table in the living room, dining room or at worst in the kitchen.

This may not create too many problems if you live on your own, but with the presence of a partner and children, problems can soon arise.

First, decide how much space you need and how much is available to you. Agree this with your family. If you don't, then your tabletop office will quickly spread, to their growing irritation.

With a little reorganisation a small bureau or desk can be fitted into most living rooms. Choose one that blends in with the decor.

Make sure that this desk has as much drawer space as possible. Working from a small desk means you have to trim filing and other paperwork to the bone. Even if you store many papers elsewhere in the house, you will want to keep at least as many of your important and useful papers near to hand as you can.

Such bureaus and desks are available from large DIY and home decoration stores, or through catalogues. Alternatively look out for a suitable one at auction sales.

Try and set up your desk away from the worst sources of disruption, such as the television, the sofa, or a frequently opened door. This generally means pushing it against a wall or into a corner. Facing a wall may feel claustrophobic at first, but it is far less distracting than staring into the middle of a room, trying not to watch the television screen you can see out of the corner of your eye.

In this position, you will probably have your back to the window. So make sure that you have a desk lamp to give you enough light to work by.

Once established in your 'lair', do everything you can to make this desk your exclusive property and guard it jealously. If your desk ends up as a general stuffing ground for others' bits and pieces, your place of work will soon become a scene of irritation.

At a very early stage of your homeworking career establish a set of 'do's' and 'don'ts' that apply to your tabletop office and when you are working from it. For more on this subject see Chapter Nine, 'How to Cope with Problems'.

If you have to work from a 'living room', then create a feeling of extra privacy by placing a shoulder-high divider or screen between your work area and the rest of the room. With some luck and a little family negotiation you may be able to leave the screen permanently in position, even adding shelves and a pinboard to it.

CASE STUDIES

Janet creates a worktop
Janet decided she wanted to use her secretarial skills and make money working from home. The trouble was she had no office.

The only place she could possibly work from in her shared house was her own room. But this was only just large enough to hold her heavy bed and an old armchair. There was absolutely no room for a desk, or for that matter anything else.

But then Janet thought of the time she had been in hospital. Hadn't the nurses wheeled a table over her bedside chair so that she could eat and write while sitting?

Wouldn't that idea work for her? Janet thought it would, but until she found such a table, she would have to compromise. A thick sheet of plywood laid across the arms of an old chair would temporarily serve the same purpose.

She would work on that, but keep her files and stationery in the bottom of the small built-in wardrobe. A wire supermarket basket could hold all the papers, cuttings and books that she needed for a particular project, so that everything was in one place.

The only problem with this system was that once she was at her 'desk' Janet found it difficult to get out of the chair. 'But that keeps me working,' she told herself. 'I just have to make sure I'm organised before I sit down, but that's a good thing too.'

Janet found her solution by racking her brains and turning the negatives of a situation into positives.

Carol's rota of workplaces

Like Janet, Carol shares a house with two other girls, who work shifts. When the pair aren't spending the day sleeping, they seem to be playing music or filling the house with friends.

That never really bothered Carol until she began to work from home as a freelance journalist. Then she suddenly found there was no space or peace and quiet to ever finish a piece of work. But that was before she became a homeworking 'gypsy'.

Two years ago Carol bought herself a laptop computer, and began asking her friends if she could work from their homes during the week. Now she has a regular rota of workplaces. Perhaps she'll spend one morning working at one house, before moving on in the afternoon to another friend's flat.

When Carol wants to print out an article or send a fax, she goes back home where the necessary equipment lurks in the bottom of her wardrobe to be brought out.

Telephone messages are left on the answer machine, taken by her fellow lodgers, or redirected to the number she is at for the day.

It's not a system that would work for everyone and Carol is fortunate that she is in a business that allows her to keep her 'home' office to a minimum. A graphic designer, for example, wouldn't really be able to take this option.

Roger's 'van' office

If you are tight on space for your new home office, let your imagination run wild, there may be a good solution staring you in the face. Take Roger, an editor who lives in a small semi-detached house in a Midland town. He desperately needed an office but couldn't think where to put one. There were no free bedrooms and with three teenagers in the house whose lives seemed to revolve around the television, there was no way he could work in the living room.

But then he saw his neighbour's family going on holiday in a camper van. Though there wasn't a lot of room inside, there was a table and you could almost stand up straight. Wouldn't that do for an office?

Roger searched through the local newspapers and Exchange and Mart looking for a cheap camper van for sale nearby. Quite soon he found one, and paid less than two hundred pounds. The van wasn't a good runner, but that didn't matter. Roger was able to drive the van into his back garden where he began to transform it into his office. Now he has a serviceable office, connected to electricity and telephone and equipped with table and shelves. He could have done the same with a small caravan.

CHECKLIST

1. Decide what room or space you are going to use for your office. Carefully measure your office and then draw the space on paper, marking any windows or doors.
2. Decide what are going to be the most used pieces of equipment and activity areas in your office. In descending order these might be: desk, computer, printer, filing cabinet, shelving, more work space, fax machine and photocopier.
3. Try and design your office so that all of the items you need are within easy reach.
4. What needs to be done to make it into an office that will work for you?
5. Decide on a specific date when you are going to complete your home office. Write it down and stick to it.
6. Having come up with what you think is a good design for your office, then come up with two or three others. Don't be satisfied with the first.
7. Visit the offices of other people who work from home, especially those who have been doing so for a while. Ask their advice and find out what are the pros and cons of different ways of working.
8. Read as many books as you can on the subject of office design. And though many of these will be on designing for the larger office, take the basic principles and apply them to your home office.
9. Make a checklist of all the things that need to be done in the office before you can really start working them there. This might include painting, filling in cracks, cleaning etc. How many of these things can be put off until you are well into your working stride? Tasks involving major work or effort, such as putting in new heating or lighting, should be put at the top of the list.

4
Furnishings and Equipment

SPOKEN FROM EXPERIENCE

'Give us the tools, and we shall finish the job.' Winston Churchill, British statesman.

'Obsession with office furnishings is often evidence that one is losing sight of objectives.' Edwin C Bliss, time management expert.

'... for want of a nail the shoe was lost; for want of a shoe the horse was lost; and for want of a horse the rider was lost.' Benjamin Franklin.

'But whether you work with computers or not, it is important to become friends with the computer and become computer literate, because the computer will permeate the whole world of work.' John Naisbitt, author of *Megatrends*.

WHAT ARE YOUR NEEDS?

How much office equipment you need depends on the nature of your business. Someone who deals in words and research will need a telephone and computer, but not a darkroom or drawing board as a photographer or designer would.

Even if you are in the fortunate position of having ample funds and love your creature comforts, do not become carried away with the prospect of working from home by splashing out on expensive equipment you do not need or that is too lavish for your real needs. Remember you are in business to make money not to spend it. However, don't let your needs become too basic.

If your business is going to flourish as you hope, then you may quickly outgrow your initial purchases leaving you either having to put up with their shortcomings or paying out in the near future for equipment better suited to your needs. This will obviously have a bad effect on your cash flow.

Always look to the future, identifying any 'production bottlenecks' that might slow you down. This applies at any stage of your business. Don't leave updating your equipment until you hit one of these production bottlenecks.

BASIC FURNITURE AND STORAGE

The three main essentials of any office are somewhere to write, somewhere to sit, and somewhere to put books and papers. You should take the time and trouble to ensure that you can do all three effectively.

Choosing a desk

Your desk is one of the most important items of office furniture. It is worth spending the time to find one that is best suited to your needs. After all, you will spend many hours sitting and working there. If you do not choose wisely at the beginning then you will soon be frustrated and annoyed by its limitations.

It doesn't really matter what your desk is made of, though most people prefer wood to metal as it feels warmer. But there are a few features you should look for:

- The desk's underside should be high enough to allow sufficient room for your legs to fit beneath without touching. You will soon become uncomfortable if you have to squeeze yourself in.

- The work surface of the desk should not be too high. For effective keyboard use the desk should be about 70cm high and should allow you to rest your forearms comfortably on the desktop. Some traditional desks used for writing are often higher than this. Use them and you will put yourself into a bad posture.

- If you use a computer, the desk should be at least 75cm deep. This not only allows the screen to be set at the optimal distance of between 35-60 centimetres away, but also prevents objects dropping off the back edge. An irritating consequence of using a shallower desk.

- Desk width is a matter of personal choice, your specific needs and the size of the room. Though a desk must give you enough space to spread papers, if it is too large there is a tendency for papers to accumulate in a clutter.

- The desktop should not have a shiny surface, otherwise light will only reflect off it causing distractions and eye-strain. Choose a top with a matt finish in a medium colour, or create this effect with a few coats of paint sealed with a matt varnish for extra toughness.

- Beware of desks that have sharp corners, particularly if metal. Even the most careful person will bash a leg on the corner of a desk from time to time and rounded edges do far less damage.

- Your desk should have plenty of drawers in a variety of depths. Shallow ones can be used for storing stationery, pens and rulers, while the deeper ones can hold files that you use frequently.

The benefits of a second desk

Many homeworkers have two desks or tables in their office. One is their standard desk at which they write and type, but the other is a larger table on which papers can be spread. This is particularly useful if you are working on a long-term project as relevant papers can be left out, rather than tidied up whenever you have to work at your main desk.

Some homeworkers make their second desk a multi-level computer table, which keeps their machine away from their main work area. If you are short on space and spend much of your time at the computer, then this could be a good buy. Basic tables can be bought for under £100.

How to make a simple DIY desk

If you cannot afford a purpose-built desk then a good substitute can be made from a flush-faced door resting on a pair of two-drawer filing cabinets, or wooden trestles. Panelled doors can be used by placing a sheet of hardboard on top. A 'door-table' also provides a quickly made and cheap second work surface.

Choosing an office chair

Your chair is perhaps the most vital piece of office equipment, as a poor purchase can badly affect your long-term health. For this reason it is best never to 'just make do'. You should go out of your way to find one that suits you, even if it is relatively expensive.

The types of office chair

There are two main kinds of chair to look at: the adjustable typist's chair and back-friendly chairs in which you kneel! These chairs consist of a fabric seat and a lower platform. To use them you simply kneel on the lower platform and sit yourself on the higher one. The chair is said to take the pressure from your back, throwing your weight forward and onto your knees and legs. These chairs are very comfortable to sit in and do relieve your back. Unfortunately they are not adjustable for height, so they may not be the first choice for working at the computer.

Typists' chairs on the other hand, allow you to carefully adjust your position so that you are comfortable and seated properly at your desk at all times. A good one should allow you to adjust not only its height but also the back support.

The seat should be covered with a porous fabric, which to put it bluntly, absorbs your sweat. And if you don't think you perspire in this region just sit on a plastic chair on a summer's day for any length of time. The results will dampen your spirits.

For extra stability, choose a typist's chair with a five-star base on castors, so that you can push yourself from one part of the office to another, rather than stand up.

Avoid chairs with seats that rise upwards at their open end. This ridge will dig into the backs of your thighs, which is uncomfortable and unhealthy.

For those who suffer from back problems, or those with the money to prevent them, there are several state-of-the-art, and therefore expensive (£300-400) chairs available. These can swivel, rock, adjust backwards and forwards, they also possess armrests that can be raised and lowered, and additional lumber support.

How to sit comfortably and healthily
To achieve the best working position, think of your chair and desk as one unit.

- When seated at your desk your feet should be resting flat on the floor, or on a footrest. Make a special point of doing this if you suffer from lower back problems.

- Both of your thighs should be comfortably supported by the seat of the chair.

- The seat should have sufficient room for you to have some movement of your hips, which should not be cramped.

- You should try to adjust your chair so that you do not slump forward while you work. This tires your shoulders, puts a strain on your spinal column, hinders your breathing and causes indigestion. And who can work at their best with all that going on?

- Constantly shift your position when you sit so that the great pressure put on your spine is temporarily relieved and redistributed.

Filing cabinets
Two or four-drawer filing cabinets are an essential item of office furniture, so don't think you won't need them. Papers multiply like rabbits.

Cabinets are available in metal or wood, but whichever you choose make sure they are sturdy. There is no need to buy new cabinets, secondhand ones are equally good, as long as they have smooth runners. Be careful where you put filing cabinets. When filled with paper they are exceptionally heavy and can put a strain on even strong floors. Upstairs offices aren't the best place for three or four of them.

Shelving
How much shelving you need depends on your type of work. However, as a

general rule your office cannot have too much. When you can, site shelving in alcoves, this is easily put up and uses otherwise sterile space. Free-standing bookcases are equally effective, just so long as they are robust.

Put at least some shelves near to your desk so that you can just reach over and grab the books you use most, such as telephone books, dictionaries and manuals rather than having to stand up and trudge to another part of the office. This is not only annoying to do, but also a great waste of time.

Secondhand furniture or new?
It's true that first impressions do count, but because there are likely to be few visitors to your home office, there is no need for vast expenditure on the most stylish furniture and equipment to impress and influence. This is particularly important if you are just starting a business as it allows you to cut costs dramatically. When your business is up and running you can splash out on more expensive items if you wish.

As long as the furniture you use is serviceable then secondhand is fine. If you need to have some office elegance, dowdy looking furniture can be easily brightened with a coat of paint or two.

Where to buy
Reasonable quality and suitable desks can be bought from large DIY stores, while Army Surplus stores carry a good stock of ex-MOD desks, noticeboards and filing cabinets. Auctions of liquidated company belongings can also produce cheap finds. They are advertised in the local, regional, daily and trade press. Take the opportunity to look around the lots before the auction begins. If you are going to bid for items then set a realistic upper price limit for yourself and stick to it.

If you do want to treat yourself to small 'luxury' items of office equipment, make sure your name appears on the lists of mail order stationery and equipment suppliers. Without the high street overheads of their retail competitors these can offer office supplies at a good discount, especially if they are having one of their periodic sales.

Avoid retailers who are dedicated to selling office furniture as their prices are generally higher. If you want to buy new, then a tour around one of the large do-it-yourself stores or low-budget furniture stores such as IKEA, should turn up good value items.

A well equipped office is a joy to work in. The item that you need is always to hand and works perfectly first time without any fuss or bother. You should do your utmost to ensure that this is the case. But be warned, it is very easy to become addicted to office equipment, such as another filing cabinet or set of pens, just because they look good or might come in useful.

Action point
Using your local papers, telephone directories and Yellow Pages make a
list of six suppliers of new and secondhand office furniture.

1._____

2._____

3._____

4._____

5._____

6._____

CHOOSING A TYPEWRITER

Every business must have some means of professionally presenting
material that will be read by others. No matter how good your
handwriting, you cannot hope to be taken seriously if you send your
letters written in longhand, so at the very least you must beg, borrow or
steal a typewriter that produces crisp characters from a fresh black, and
only black, ribbon.

- Preferably this machine should be electric as this produces a more
  even character on the page than a manual typewriter. In business
  appearance counts for much.

- Choose a machine with a self-correcting key. This gives a far neater
  correction than covering your mistakes with Tippex.

- If you can afford it, buy a typewriter with a memory. This holds
  your text, perhaps a few lines or maybe a whole page, in 'limbo', so if
  you do make a mistake you can alter it before committing your
  words to paper. The more expensive the machine the more likely it is
  to have a larger memory, capable of storing all of a short document
  or letter.

- Look for a machine with 'coded keys' that allow you to quickly
  move around the page, from top to bottom and left to right.

- Though many typewriters are similar, not all 'feel' the same so try
  several before buying. And don't just stand embarrassed in front of
  it, tap a few keys and say you'll have it. Use the typewriter as it is
  meant to be used, with you sitting down in front of it. If the store or
  shop won't let you do this, go elsewhere.

CHOOSING A COMPUTER

Though typewriters were once an absolute necessity, in recent years they have been superseded by computers which are now the modern workhorses of nearly all small businesses. So even if you are a paragon of typing virtue, fast and accurate, plump for a computer, it will seriously improve your productivity.

For comparatively little cost the homeworker can equip themselves with a powerful machine that offers many advantages. For this reason no apologies are made for writing here about computers at length and in detail.

What types of computers are there?
There are two basic computer systems, IBM compatible machines (such as Amstrad, Compaq, Dell and Tandon) and the Apple Macintosh. Not long ago the 'Apple Mac' was first choice if you wanted good computer graphics, complicated page layouts, or needed to mix text and graphics. IBM compatible machines were more likely to be used for number crunching, searching information and wordprocessing. However, the advent of Windows software (the programs that tell computers what to do) means that IBM compatible computers can now compete in this area.

What makes up a computer system?
Computers consist of a keyboard, a Central Processing Unit (CPU) which is the electronic heart of the machine, and a monitor on which words and graphics are displayed. These items are known as 'hardware'.

This hardware, specifically the CPU, reads a 'program' which tells it what tasks the computer must do, wordprocessing for instance. The computer has an ability to temporarily 'remember' this information in its Random Access Memory (RAM) but suffers from immediate amnesia when the power is switched off. So to store information permanently information is stored on either a floppy disk or a hard disk. Both the programs and the information that your computer generates are stored on the disks in files.

Floppy disks are now generally 3½" wide. These are pushed into slots at the front of the machine where they are 'read' by the computer. Floppy disks can store a considerable amount of information, around one hundred and fifty A4 pages of single-spaced text. With machines that do not have a hard disk, a floppy must be inserted each time the computer is 'booted up' or started, to make it work. A much easier solution is to have a machine with a hard disk which lives permanently inside.

Hard disks make life easier because they can contain a large number of programs and data files so there is no need to slot in a different floppy when you want to use another program. And depending on its capacity, a hard disk may hold thirty to a hundred times more information than a floppy disk. Indeed, some computer programs will only run on a hard disk. A 80K hard disk will be large enough for most homeworkers, unless you want to do desktop publishing or hold vast amounts of information in a database.

What to look for when buying a computer

Buy a selection of computer magazines and see what machines they recommend that are within your budget. Some dealers advertise their machines at substantial discounts, often several hundred pounds, so look for bargains. Generally the more heavily advertised the computer the more it will cost and besides, heavy advertising and a high price are no guarantee of quality.

Do not buy your computer from a dealer simply because he is nearest and you can't be bothered to shop around. You want a store that will give good advice and help *after* you have bought from them. Give the cold shoulder to any dealer who is unwilling to make time to talk to you before you buy. He certainly will ignore you once he has your money.

In general, the faster your computer performs tasks, the more expensive it will be. Most accounting and wordprocessing packages don't need very fast machines, but certain types of program, large databases and accounting spreadsheets, do need the extra speed if you are not to be left twiddling your thumbs for thirty seconds.

It's best not to buy dedicated wordprocessors; though they are good at this job, they cannot perform other computing functions. You pay almost the same money as for a computer but have a much less powerful machine.

Technology is moving so fast that new machines are coming out all the time so don't hang around waiting for next week's new 'singing and all dancing computer' to come out otherwise you'll end up never buying a computer. If you decide to buy a computer, don't wait around, go and buy it now.

The monitor

Though a colour monitor for your computer is visually more exciting, monochrome ones are adequate for most people and save money. Unless you are going to be desktop publishing, there is no need for a high resolution monitor. Before you buy your machine try and see if text is hard to read on the screen; if it is then you will soon suffer from eye-strain.

The keyboard

The way a keyboard feels is a matter for your personal choice and tastes.

Try out a keyboard for as long as possible before buying it. Though the QWERTY format is standard, there are alternative types of keyboard with different layouts or designs to minimise the unnatural bending of the wrists required when working at a conventional keyboard. If a keyboard irritates you slightly after ten minutes because of a rough surface, or the position of its keys, you can be sure you won't ever become used to it. Reject it.

The printer
Unlike a typewriter, a computer needs a separate printing unit to produce 'hard copy'. There are several types of computer printer, each with their own advantages and disadvantages.

Dot matrix printers are cheap and sufficient for most tasks. They produce two types of lettering: draft and Near Letter Quality (NLQ). Printing in draft mode is fast but of quite low quality, while NLQ mode looks far better, but takes twice as long to produce. Dot matrix printers can print out graphics, such as tables, graphs and pictures.

A better alternative is the bubble or inkjet printer. Quiet, fast and cheap these give a printout that has almost the clarity and sharpness of a laser printer. Top of the range machines are also capable of printing in colour.

Somewhat more expensive are laser printers which can now be bought for £400-500. However, they offer very high quality printouts, including graphics. They work in a similar manner to a photocopier and require a toner cartridge.

Choosing software
Three main types of software will interest the homeworker—wordprocessors, databases and accounting spreadsheets. Of these the most widely used and useful will undoubtedly be the wordprocessor.

What is a wordprocessor?
A vast number of wordprocessors are on the market. They range from the basic and cheap to the complicated and highly expensive. With varying degrees of sophistication, they all do the same thing, which is to turn your computer into a highly flexible and powerful electronic typewriter... only more so. They allow even the world's worst typist to create a professional looking letter or document by editing their work in a simple way.

Unlike a typewriter, even one with a memory of a few hundred words, a wordprocessor does not set your words in stone. What you type is held in temporary storage until you are ready to save your pearls of wisdom to a floppy or hard disk, or send them to your printer. All this means you can change your mind at any time while you type. You can remove a sentence or add a single word, while mistakes can be erased with just a few keystrokes. Blocks of text can be moved from one place to another in the document and even between different files.

Because of this ability to change, re-use or retrieve what you have previously written, a wordprocessor makes you more productive. This is not the case with a typewriter. Once you have typed out a word there is no chance of using it elsewhere. It has gone forever.

How to choose a wordprocessor

Any wordprocessor you buy should allow you to italicise, embolden or underline words, lines or blocks of text. Buy one that highlights or otherwise prominently marks these 'enhanced' blocks of text.

In addition it should be able to find specific words in a document text and replace them with others, check your spelling, number the pages when you print out and count the number of words you have written.

One particularly useful feature is a mailmerge facility. This lets you take addresses from a database file and 'stick' them onto a form letter which is held elsewhere.

Many modern wordprocessors are WYSIWYG (What You See Is What You Get) which means that what you see on the screen is the way that the document will be printed out. This gives you better control over the design and layout of your letters and reports before they are committed to paper.

When choosing a wordprocessor look for one that can convert what it creates into ASCII format, which is like Esperanto for computers, an international language that lets one wordprocessor read files from another. This means that you can swap information with other people and their machines.

If you produce a lot of articles, stories or reports you can buy style checkers which work in tandem with your wordprocessor. Style checking software can discover errors in your grammar or phrasing and tell you if you are being too highbrow, too technical or formal for your audience.

Before buying software try and test it out first. You will probably need to spend an hour or more to find out whether you really like a particular package. One way of doing this is to use shareware, which is the computer world's equivalent of the honesty box. You buy the software, a wordprocessor for instance, for just a few pounds, try it out, and if you like it register as a user and send the balance of the payment. You should not keep on using the program if you are not going to send money. Many shareware programs are very good and generally cheaper than the commercial software widely advertised. At the very least read as many reviews from computer magazines as you can, it may stop you making an expensive mistake.

How to choose a database

A computer database is simply a collection of information organised so that it can be divided into groups, merged with other documents, or searched for data that meets special criteria. This information can be telephone numbers, addresses, names, contacts, places, or ideas.

The simplest databases are known as 'flat-files'. These hold data in a rigid format which you create. They are much like a card index which can be ordered and shuffled. However, you cannot link information on different 'cards' or files. They are perfect for simply holding facts and figures that you need to call up from time to time.

Relationship databases, on the other hand, are more powerful and flexible. They can link information together that is held in different files, so you can cross-reference numerous items. As you would expect they are more expensive than flat-file databases.

How to choose a spreadsheet

Spreadsheets are to numbers as wordprocessors are to words. They let you move, manipulate, erase and copy numbers so that you can manage your budget and better control your financial affairs.

By hand, preparing a spreadsheet is a time-consuming process that requires a lot of calculations with pencil and calculator. With a computer spreadsheet you can dramatically speed up your book-keeping. The computer will almost instantly add up columns of figures, calculate averages and substitute new values if you make a mistake. It will also let you quickly manipulate the data using financial formulae to see how well your business is doing.

Most homeworkers will not need a very powerful spreadsheet, a simple accounting package should be enough and there are many of these on the market. Choose one that has a reputation for being easy to use. Some of the more powerful spreadsheets will only work off a hard drive.

One particularly useful facility is the ability to create different 'windows' through which you can look at different sections of the spreadsheet at one time.

Caring for your computer

It is worth looking after your computer, especially if it has a hard disk. If your computer 'crashes' you will be unable to access the disk and are likely to lose a vast amount of data, which could do irreparable harm to your business. Though it applies to medium to large companies, a recent US survey observes that of the companies who experienced a computer disaster, eighty per cent (80%) of them went out of business within eighteen months.

How to care for your computer

If your machine withstands the unpacking from its box and stays up and running for several months without causing any problems, then it should continue to operate without problems for several years, perhaps even five or six. So that any bugs show themselves quickly, at first try and keep the machine running for long periods at a time. Help to ensure your machine stays trouble-free by taking some simple precautions:

- Don't turn your computer on and off unnecessarily. The electrical surge this produces is more harmful than keeping your computer running all day. Personal computers don't use a great deal of electricity, so turning them off when you go onto another job won't save much money anyway.

- Check the fuse in your computer's plug. The chances are that it is 13 amps. This is too high. Switch to a maximum of 5 amps, this protects both your computer and your electricity in the event of a surge. Remember, a blown fuse costs only pence, a blown computer may be your business.

- Don't block any of the machine's air vents. The build up of heat can affect components as can being too close to a radiator. The frequent local changes in temperature can eventually warp the circuit boards and separate the electrical joints.

- Keep the keyboard and back of the computer well cleaned so that dust is not blown inside the machine. Dust covers are available for both keyboard and the main machine. Use them when you have finished for the day.

- Be careful about drinking near the keyboard. Moisture and electronics simply do not mix. Plastic shields can be placed over the keys to give protection. If you have plants in your office either take them out to spray, or keep them well away from the computer.

- Don't smoke near your computer. Even these minute particles can affect the data that is kept on your floppy disks and hard drive.

- Don't put your computer near to a doorway or anywhere it could be knocked.

- Periodically check that ribbon cables, the flat electrical straps that are often used to connect a computer to a modem or printer, aren't kinked. Estimates put about 15% of computer failures down to this.

- Disks are available which are designed to clean the floppy disk drive. Their effectiveness is questionable and some computer experts believe they can cause more problems than they solve.

- If for no apparent reason your computer throws a wobbly or loses data, the culprit may be a 'spike' or fluctuation in the electricity supply. Heavy machinery starting up nearby could be one reason. Spike suppressors sold through computer dealers should remedy the problem.

How to care for computer disks

Even though some floppy disks are quite rigid, they are still fragile commodities. If they become damaged or corrupted then all the information held on them—your hard work—could be lost.

Keeping vital information on just one disk is courting disaster. Your files need to be 'backed-up' from time to time, onto other floppy disks. Once you have backed up your copies, you should put 'write protect' tabs on them. These are sticky bits of tape that cover the notch on the side of the disk so that you cannot write over any of its contents. As an added insurance it is worth making printed copies of your work.

There are four main enemies of disks: cigarettes, coffee, cats and kids. Fingers should never be placed near or on the exposed magnetic surfaces of a disk. Likewise strong magnetic fields, such as you might find near televisions and telephones, should be kept away from them. For the same reason, never lean a disk against the monitor screen, the electro-magnetic emissions from it, though low-level, are still sufficient to destroy or rearrange data.

Don't leave disks lying around on your desk. Put them away in their sleeves and disk box when you are finished with them.

Never remove a disk from the computer when the drive it's in is still running. This corrupts data and could eventually ruin the expensive drive. A warning light usually goes out when the drive has finished turning. Only then take out a floppy disk.

Use only one floppy disk per job. A job could be all the work for one client, a novel, or all the letters to your favourite aunt.

Once a day, and at least once a week take the trouble to delete unwanted files from floppy disks and hard drives, while their contents are fresh in your mind.

Save your work frequently—every ten to fifteen minutes. Then, even if you are a fast typist, if the electricity fails or the computer breaks down, you should only lose five or six hundred words, not an entire morning's work. Save your files to back-up disks at least twice a day. This doesn't take long, and you really are far better off being safe than sorry.

Computer viruses

Though computer viruses do grab the attention of the media, they are not common and most computer users will never experience their ill effects.

A virus is a malicious program that slows down your computer or damages information held on the disks. They are passed on between computers via infected disks or public databases of information. If you only buy software from reputable sources, never swap disks with anyone else, or connect to an electronic database, you are exceptionally unlikely to 'catch a virus'.

If you do exchange disks regularly it is worth investing in anti-virus software that will 'disinfect' your machine. There are a number of such programs around and they can give peace of mind.

What is a maintenance contract and do you need one?

Should your computer break down, a maintenance contract enables you to call out an engineer within a pre-set time to fix it. Some contracts also provide a replacement machine whilst yours is being repaired. Maintenance contracts are expensive, so compare the prices offered by various companies, but it is not always wise to go for the cheapest contract. You want the company to still be in business when you need them, provide high quality technical support and answer your call as quickly as possible. Well established firms should be able to do this, cut-price smaller companies may not be so reliable.

Why a second computer is no luxury

If you rely on a computer for your work then what are you going to do if it goes wrong and you have to finish that report by tomorrow? A maintenance contract is one option already discussed, but contracts are expensive.

Therefore consider buying another machine as a back-up. Make sure that it is compatible with your main machine and that you can exchange disks. It's true that this machine will sit around doing nothing most of the time, but it will certainly give peace of mind.

And if your main computer does break down you will be able to have it repaired at a more leisurely and less expensive pace, while you can keep working on the second machine without breaking your flow. Use your second machine periodically to check it out.

Buying another machine need not be expensive. You can save hundreds of pounds by buying secondhand at an auction or through a private sale. Remember at auctions you may knock 40-50% off the computer's price, but VAT and a buyer's commission must be added to this. When you buy in this way it is a good idea to take along with you someone who knows about computers.

Learning more about computers

Many novice computer users find that the best way to learn about their machine and what it can do is simply to sit down in front of it and make mistakes. Don't worry, you won't break the computer.

However, if you need moral and technical support, then most local authorities run computer and wordprocessing courses. Enrol and get a feel for the machines before you buy one of your own.

For those who like to pick others' brains, it is worth joining a user's group for your type of computer. Here you will find varying degrees of expertise, but one member or another will be able to solve your problems and offer a guiding hand. Your local computer shop may have details of the various groups who do sometimes advertise in computer magazines.

Some of the computer magazines run regular series of beginners' articles which explain the fundamentals of computers and computing.

Every homeworker who is serious about their business and produces a reasonable amount of written material should learn to touch-type. Courses are available at most local authority education centres, but if you have the determination why not teach yourself. There are many good typing books to help you on your way. You do not need to become a very fast typist, just a competent one with a reasonable speed.

DO YOU NEED A FAX?

The world of the home-based worker has been revolutionised by the arrival of low-cost fax machines, which are really remote photocopiers that allow the transmission of a document from one place to another via the telephone line.

The advantages of a fax are that it is cheap to use and fast. While sending a first class letter costs at present 25p without a guarantee that it will arrive the next day, a document can be faxed almost instantaneously elsewhere for just a fifth of that or less.

There are two types of fax machines that will interest the homeworker. These are Group 3 and 4. Group 3 faxes are the industry standard, but Group 4 faxes send faster, but they require a digital telephone network which isn't available everywhere in the country.

Under ideal circumstances, an A4 sheet of typed text takes between fifteen and twenty seconds on a Group 3 machine, though this will depend on the speed of the receiving fax.

It is worth buying a fax machine that sends documents at different resolutions, which are generally standard to fine. Standard resolution sends the document through at a faster rate but with a slight loss of clarity, while fine resolution shows greater detail but takes longer to send.

Such refinements as document feeders, cutters that automatically chop the incoming page to A4 length, and memories that hold fax numbers are all time saving and useful but add to the price.

Combined fax, telephone and answer machines are also available. These packages offer better value for money than buying all of the pieces separately, but make such that each component part does what you want it to.

If you fax over an order, you should follow up with written confirmation by post. Faxes on fax paper fade with time, so take copies of them before storing, or buy a fax that uses plain paper.

If your fax and telephone share the same telephone line, then buy a 'fax switch'. This box of electronics recognises whether the incoming call is from another fax or a telephone and directs it accordingly. This not only saves you lifting the receiver to be blasted by the banshee scream of a fax, but means that callers don't have to ring you up to tell you to switch over to your fax.

PHOTOCOPYING

Every business needs to photocopy documents from time to time, but only you know whether you really need a photocopier in your office.

Questions and answers

1. *How many photocopies do you make each week?* If you only make a small number of copies every few weeks then you don't really need a copier. The cost and inconvenience of finding one in town outweighs the cost of buying a copier.

2. *How much time do you waste going to find a photocopy machine?* If you make copies regularly and find yourself having to make treks into town at inconvenient times then a copier in your office would be of help.

3. *How many more photocopies would you make if you had a machine on the premises?* If you find yourself spending a lot of time making notes from books, or magazines you should consider getting a copier.

Most homeworkers have no need of a large high-volume photocopier with lots of facilities. A basic machine is sufficient as long as it is easy to operate and produces a good crisp copy that is reliable. Usually small copiers only allow copies of documents sized A4 or less. The ability to copy A3 paper, though useful, is one that most people won't use often. If you need to copy a larger size then you can always do it bit by bit and stick the pieces together. Most cheaper copiers copy on a ratio of 1:1—the copy is the exact size of the original, however more sophisticated models are able to enlarge and reduce.

The quality of your photocopies is dependent on the toner, either black powder or liquid. You should buy a machine that holds the toner in a disposable cartridge, which is just slotted into the machine when required. A cartridge lasts for perhaps 3,000 copies, which will see many homeworkers through the year.

Like other capital expenditure on equipment the cost of a photocopier is tax deductible if you buy it, as is the rental charge if you decide to hire. If you do hire, be careful about signing a service contract that ties you to a particular dealer for years ahead. You must be able to break the contract if the service you receive is unreliable or poor, and go elsewhere. Do business with a well established office supply company whose reliability and service you can trust.

If you hire, then check what is included in the agreement between you and the hire purchase company who finance the deal. For instance, are spare parts and toner included in the cost-per-copy price? If not then the costs will rise and need to be added in. Check before you sign any rental agreement.

CHOOSING A PHONE SYSTEM

The homeworker's phone is a lifeline to the world. Of course the most basic of phones serves its purpose, however, for dedicated homeworking a more sophisticated instrument is needed.

A phone with a ten or twenty number memory is a useful time saver. It means you don't have to look up a number and can dial it by pressing one button rather than ten. Additional facilities that may interest you are: a secrecy button that lets you speak to someone in your office without being overheard; a call timer; and a digital display that shows the number you are calling.

Homeworkers should make use of BT's extra 'Star' services. Amongst the most useful of these is 'call diversion' which directs an incoming call to wherever you may be, and 'call waiting' which informs you that another caller is waiting to speak when you are already on the line.

Consider investing in a portable phone, then if you are in the midst of a household chore or taking a break, you can quickly talk to a calling client without having to make a spring for the phone in an upstairs office. Letting the phone ring too long creates a bad impression and could lose you business if a client hangs up.

If you require more than one phone on a line, it is easy enough to install an extension socket, though don't put more than four phones on any one line as this can affect the ringer circuits.

What about Mercury?

It is worth buying a Mercury compatible phone, because if your area is not yet linked with the Mercury phone system it probably will be before you are in the market for a new phone. Anyone able to should subscribe to the Mercury phone system, the only phone company offering a rival telecommunications service to BT. By subscribing, phone users can make considerable cost cuts (10-15%) on long distance calls.

No special line is required, but Mercury subscribers pay a small annual charge for which they are given a personal code that is keyed into their phones. Mercury Smart Sockets are available which plug into a standard BT socket and which automatically route your long distance calls and international calls away from BT and onto the cheaper Mercury network.

Do you need a second phone line?

The serious homeworker should put in an extra phone line which can be used either for a fax or an extra phone. This ensures that your business is never interrupted because an incoming or outgoing domestic call goes on too long, something which can reach interminable lengths if a teenage son or daughter is involved.

With a dedicated business line you are never in two minds as to who is on the other end of your phone. A call on one line is business, on the other line it is personal.

A further advantage of a business line is that you are given a *Yellow Pages* listing, and are entitled to financial compensation for every day if a fault on a business line is not fixed by the end of the working day and also if you can prove that you have lost business through a delay in installing and repairing a line.

Using your telephone number to sell

Though BT allocates you a telephone number, they will attempt to change it to suit your needs. In this way you can create a more memorable telephone number, especially if you can find a direct link between the number and your service or product. Unless you are wanting a very unusual telephone number such as 444 444, then this will cost no more than the standard charge for a number change.

Do you need an answer machine?

Yes. Once an answer machine was a luxury, now it is an essential business tool and the home-based worker cannot afford to be without one. Undoubtedly there are some people who call and will not leave messages on your answer machine. They may not give you their business, but many others will leave messages that result in fresh work.

There are many machines on the market and it is worth shopping around to find the best deal. Once basic devices, answer machines now abound with extra features, though really there are only a few that should interest you.

- All machines should indicate that there are messages waiting to be heard, though some go further by showing the number of messages.

- Choose a machine with remote interrogation. This lets you listen to your messages when you are miles away at another phone. It is useful when you are expecting a call, or need to deal quickly with unexpected bits of business that you wouldn't otherwise know about until you returned home and checked the messages.

What should your answer machine say?

When you are out of the office the answer machine is your secretary, and like any good secretary it must answer the phone courteously and in keeping with your business image.

The message should be interesting, professional, friendly and depending on your business, creative. Sound effects can be effective as long as they are not overdone. They should never obscure the information you want the caller to hear. Unlike other areas of business you can be funny with an answer machine message, but only you know how far you can go. You would expect the message from a television comedy writer to be humorous, but if you are a private detective that is far from the right image to convey.

For security's sake, don't say on the message that you are out. Burglars do listen to answerphones, so be ambiguous as to why you can't come to the phone. Perhaps you could offer other reasons why you can't pick up the phone. For instance, a photographer's message might run along the lines of, 'Sorry I can't pick up the phone right now, I'm probably in the darkroom. Just leave your name and number and I'll get back to you as soon as I can.'

Female voices can give a softer tone to an answer machine message. If you are a particularly gruff-voiced male, or feel that your voice doesn't have the right quality, ask your wife or a female friend to be the 'voice' of your business. This also has the advantage of suggesting that you are more than a one-man, or one-woman band.

Keep the message as short as possible, callers easily become bored and after all they are the ones who are paying to listen to your monologue. Try to change your message regularly so that frequent callers aren't bombarded with the same words.

OTHER OFFICE ACCESSORIES

You may have all of the large pieces of your office equipment, but there are numerous, smaller items that do make office life easier. Some of these will be suitable for your business, others won't.

Document holder

A useful accessory that holds papers vertically in front of you so that you don't have to constantly switch your gaze between desktop and computer screen. The document holder should be positioned at the same distance, height and angle as the computer screen so you are not continually re-focusing your eyes.

Electronic calculator

Though a small pocket calculator is useful, a more robust machine with a paper readout is better still, especially for doing accounts, because you can keep a double check on sums.

Tape recorder

A non-essential item of office equipment, but highly useful. A hand-held recorder is convenient and efficient for making notes when driving in the car and can be used with equal effect in the home. You can also use the machine to record telephone conversations to ensure that all details of a brief, contract, interview or commission are noted, but never wholly rely on the recorder. Take written notes as well.

If you intend to record from the phone you will need a special microphone with a rubber sticker to fit it to the receiver. A little perseverance is needed to find the ideal position so that both your voice and the caller's are clear and loud. Mark the place, as the microphone is sure to come adrift from the receiver and you won't want to go through the procedure again.

The quality of recording achieved with a stick-on microphone is generally adequate, but for better recordings, a recorder dedicated to the purpose can be bought for around £100. Some of these machines generate a low beep at regular intervals which theoretically informs the caller that the conversation is being recorded. But this is only a matter of courtesy. There are no legal problems about taping a telephone conversation for your own use and many banks, stockbrokers and financial institutions do it as a matter of course. You do *not* have to tell the other person that the conversation is being recorded.

Franking machines

Franking machines free the tongue from stamp licking, by printing the amount of postage required, and an advertising message if you wish, onto your envelopes. The total postage cost is recorded on a meter which must be periodically taken to a Post Office where the funds are recredited. Some sophisticated machines allow you to do this automatically using new technology.

Unless you produce vast quantities of mail each day you don't need one. They do give a professional appearance to your mailings but this is more than outweighed by their expense—£600 or more.

General office supplies

These are some of the items that you are likely to use on a regular basis, so keep them near at hand.

Diary	Sticky tape
Calendar	Blu-Tack
Letter opener	Glue
Notepad	Sharp-bladed knife
Paper clips	Scissors
Pens and pencils	Tippex and thinner
Highlighter pen	Sticky labels
Eraser	Wastepaper basket
Ruler	Envelopes
Stapler and staples	Stamps
Staple remover	Filing materials

These items you will use less regularly, but make sure you have them around, otherwise you will need them at a crucial moment, probably when the shops are closed.

Printer ribbons	Plugs
Small screwdriver	Padded envelopes
Paper punch	Parcel tape
Formatted computer disks	Bulbs for desk and room lights
Toner for photocopier and printer	Cassette tapes
Electric fuses	

CASE HISTORIES

Edward the market researcher

Edward is a homeworking market researcher who has been doing things the same way for years and sees no reason to change. He is a highly conscientious man and none of the clients for whom he works get anything but his best efforts.

Edward could farm out all of his typing, but he likes to do it all himself. 'It gives me more control,' he says, 'and when I'm typing I often think of new ideas which I can incorporate in my reports.'

But because he is a perfectionist, if Edward makes a mistake he re-types a whole section which he admits does slow him down. Edward always works hard at finishing his work well before the deadline so that he has time to send a report in by post. He has thought about using a computer, but doesn't think he'd 'get on with one' at the grand old age of forty-nine.

Edward works long hours, using the same desk and chair that he's always used. He has meant to replace both of them, but has never quite got around to it. And yes, he does suffer from a bit of backache now and then after he's been working for a few hours, but he puts that down to the gardening he did at the weekend or 'just old age'. On the whole Edward does a very good job, but he does make life hard for himself.

Madeline's productivity

Another researcher, Madeline, is fifty-two and being open minded, is the opposite of Edward. She quickly saw the advantages of using a computer. Now she produces reports which are similar to Edward's, only she does this much faster.

'I never waste a word as I used to with a typewriter,' she says. 'I tend to think of it as recycling my sentences, because I can keep on re-using them. When I've written the first draft of a report I simply use it as a skeleton for the next one. Whereas with a typewriter I had to re-type everything again for the second draft, even if it were only a little different from the previous one.

'And now that I have the fax, I've bought myself a little extra time, because I don't have to allow for the post, or even taking a report into a client's office.'

Edward would be shocked to see that Madeline produces 25% more than him during the working week.

CHECKLIST

Make a list of all the equipment you think you will need to run your business profitably and productively. You do not need to include every last pen and pencil.

Cost each item. What is the total?_____

How does this compare with the money available for your business? What is the difference?_____

Can you borrow any of the items you need to reduce your start-up costs? Which ones?_____

Are there any items that you can put off buying in the immediate future? Which ones?_____

5
Teleworking

SPOKEN FROM EXPERIENCE

Teleworking is 'rather like going to work on the telephone line rather than the Piccadilly Line'. Iain Vallance, BT Chairman.

'By the end of the century 70% of jobs will be cerebral (knowledge information) jobs, not manual jobs: a complete switch from 100 years ago when over 70% of all jobs were manual.' Dutch survey on the nature of work.

'I'm in contact with the other region via the electronic mail and I'm never off the phone. I'm dealing with people all the time, so it's very friendly.' Audrey Biddle, teleworker.

In theory over half of Britain's workers could be 'telecommuters'.

WHAT IS TELEWORKING?

Teleworking or telecommuting means using one computer to send and receive information to and from another. You can do this no matter where you live, be it Swansea in Wales or Swansea in Tasmania, as long as you are connected by phone line then the computers can 'talk' and the world really does become your oyster.

In Britain an estimated 500,000 full-time workers already telecommute. Another 1.5 million do so part-time. The numbers are set to grow as increasingly the economy looks as though it is going to be made up of far smaller business units, many of them one (two)man bands. By the beginning of the next century, according to the Henley Centre for Forecasting, more than 10 million will be working from home, either full- or part-time.

Why telework?
If you work from home, there are two main ways in which teleworking can benefit you.

First, you can exchange information with colleagues, suppliers or customers. Essentially any document, article, financial report or computer graphics can be sent from one computer to another. By teleworking you can do this quickly and accurately and without the need to re-type information. Such time saving can be particularly attractive to potential clients.

Second, you can make use of some of the world's greatest information sources and libraries. These electronic databases contain a wealth of information on virtually every subject under the sun. If you want to find something out then the chances are that the information will be held on a database that you can call up.

The importance of databases

Estimates put the number of such databases worldwide at around five thousand, with five hundred of them being British based. Some of these deal specifically with a single subject, for instance, coffee production or electronics, while others are gigantic electronic encyclopaedias, only better, because they contain up-to-the-minute information on a great array of topics.

Through these you can explore a worldwide range of daily newspapers, make financial assessments of companies, check on the availability of business grants, peruse the Financial Times index, make flight or hotel reservations around the globe and do much, much more.

For researchers, writers, editors and business people they are gold mines, where nuggets of data that would be found only by a long and difficult search elsewhere, can quickly be discovered.

Subscribing to databases

If you just want to send and receive information from a colleague then all you and your workmate need are a computer, modem and communications software. You need nothing else.

However, if you want to use the electronic databases you need the help of a third party because you will have to subscribe to one of the network services, such as CompuServe, which act as entry points to many databases and reference sources.

To use them you will have to pay a small registration fee, plus connection and communication fees every time that you use their system. When you register you will be given a personal identification number and password for you to use. You should keep these secure otherwise someone else could run up very high charges in your name.

On-line costs

Some databases are free, most are not. You must either subscribe to them in advance or are billed for the length of time that you spend searching through them. Charges can be high, with on-line costs (the time you spend connected to the computer) running at perhaps more than £100 an hour!

On top of this there are the telephone charges that you incur, which of course are hefty if you are accessing a database in the United States. Generally however, you can reduce your telephone charges by linking into a nearby access point, so that for British databases, wherever they are, you are only billed for local and not long distance calls.

Though this sounds very expensive, databases not only supply you with information that you would not find elsewhere but can be a highly cost-effective means of research.

A little preparatory work before you go on-line can sharply reduce your costs. The wealth of data can otherwise be overwhelming and the last thing you want is to be left wondering what to do and where to go when telephone and database charges are mounting by the second.

The first step is to know how the database you are entering functions and is structured. Some databases and system supply manuals describing the layout of the database and likely sources of information. It is also worth contacting user groups who can share their experiences with you, which should save you time and money. The basic rule when using the databases is to find what you want and get out as fast as possible. Wise database users literally just grab the information they want, sucking or 'downloading' it into their own machine. Only later when they have left the database do they read the information at their leisure. Likewise if you want to send information to someone else then you should prepare the file before you go on-line.

WHAT YOU NEED TO BE A TELEWORKER

Once you have a computer it is easy to become a teleworker, all you need are a few additional pieces of equipment and a little grasp of computer jargon, which can easily be acquired.

The modem

The first extra item required is a modem—a box of electronics that either sits near your computer, or slots inside it (an internal modem card). The modem, on one side is connected to your computer, and on the other to the phone line. Modems work by converting the information that your computer sends to it into small packets which can be sent down the telephone line. Likewise it handles the packets of information it receives from another computer, first by welcoming the other computer with a 'handshake' before handing on the information to your own.

A modem can work at different speeds, that is how fast it can send these packets of information down the telephone line. The faster it can do this, the more expensive it will be to buy, however you do save on telephone costs because it doesn't take so long to send.

However, one problem of a high-speed modem is that the faster you send information, the more likely a 'dirty' phone line is to corrupt it, or lose your connection on the phone line.

Any modem that you choose should be Hayes compatible as this is the 'industry' standard.

Communications software

Your modem does not work alone, but in conjunction with communications (comms) software which is loaded into your computer. Comms software has the task of manipulating and preparing the data in your computer so that it can be sent to the modem.

As with other software, if possible try out different programs and find one that you are comfortable with and is very easy to use. This is particularly important because you do not want to be fumbling around, uncertain how to use the program when you are connected to the phone line.

If you intend to do a lot of teleworking, consider installing another phone line. After all how is anyone going to be able to call you if your line is constantly engaged?

WILL IT WORK FOR YOU?

Despite its huge potential for finding information, and quickly and accurately sending information from one place to another, not every homeworker will be interested in using their computer to telework. By now you should have a good idea whether you will be able to benefit from what it has to offer. If you never have a need to shift or gather information, then it is not really for you. But before you think that the world of databases and teleworking cannot offer you help in the day-to-day running of your business, there are a couple of services you may be interested in.

Homebanking

Using your computer you can also take advantage of various homebanking schemes. For instance, the Bank of Scotland runs a system known as Home and Office Banking Service (HOBS) through which you can carry out most ordinary banking activities such as the payment of bills and transfers between accounts.

HOBS lets you do this at any time so that you do not have to make time-consuming trips into town and can keep an constant eye on a rapidly changing account. However, if you want to pay in money then you must still go and queue in person.

CASE HISTORIES

Mary and CompuServe

Mary, the freelance journalist, has suggested a story idea to a newspaper editor who has given her the OK to write the piece, but only speculatively. Mary knows he will buy the article but only if she gives it some extra interest and topicality.

She roughs out the first draft for the article using the reference books on her shelves, but thinks the piece is lacking a little something. Mary subscribes to CompuServe, one of the largest computerised information services, so she decides to check out one of the general databases that holds copies of many American magazines and newspapers, such as the New York Times, where Mary is pretty certain she'll find the sort of up-to-date information she needs to really 'lift' her article.

Within a few minutes Mary is logged into the American database, which she has used before. She does find what she's looking for, quickly grabs it and logs off the database. Now she not only has the latest facts on her subject, but one or two interesting titbits that she'd never even dreamt existed.

When she has written up the story on her wordprocessor Mary sends the article down the phone line, using her modem, to another computer at the editorial office. Just as is happening in many industries, editors appreciate Mary's commitment to new technology because it saves them time as they don't have to type up her manuscript and editing work can begin immediately on screen. Given the chance they will choose her in preference to a writer of equal ability who has to post or fax in articles that have to be re-typed.

Mary wins the business because she is a 'teleworker' and the cost of using her computer to access databases is an acceptable business cost. All in all, she was on-line for about six minutes which meant the telephone charges were about £1 and database fees about £5. With Mary rating her own time at £20 an hour these six minutes cost her £8.00!

That may seem a lot to pay for such a short period of research, but contrast that with someone who doesn't go on-line.

Richard's experience

Richard is researching the same subject as Mary and he also intends to send the finished article to the same editor. Fortunately, Richard is within a short drive of a very good library which he knows should have the information he wants. He thinks that it will only take him five minutes to get the information that he needs, but it isn't particularly convenient for him to go into town right now but he can't move the article forward unless he does. So there's nothing for it.

Richard does quickly find the information that he wants, but the drive to and from the library, including finding a parking space, takes forty minutes. Back home Richard soon finishes the article and faxes it off, confident that the editor will use it.

But when he checks, he finds that the work of another freelancer has already been accepted. The editor tells Richard that her article had not only come in about an hour earlier, but seemed more up-to-date and with a sharper edge to it. Richard just has to shrug his shoulder, and puts this down to a bit of 'bad luck'.

But Richard's bad luck has still cost him. He also rates his time at £20 per hour so his forty-five minute research trip costs him £15 in time plus £3 in petrol. A total of £19.00, more than double Mary's costs, and no work at the end of it.

Jon uses a telecottage

Jonathan has just set up as consultant working from home, though to do that he has had to begin with the barest minimum of equipment because he doesn't have a lot of start-up capital. He does have a computer but not a decent printer or desktop publishing software, which is a slight problem since Jonathan wants to create high quality and well presented documents. Fortunately, there is a telecottage nearby, which is a 'community office' which has lots of equipment (including a top of the range laser printer but also dtp software and the staff to teach him how to use it) which can be rented and used very cost effectively. Jonathan uses the telecottage regularly, working with more and more of the equipment. He even uses the telecottage's on-line telecommunications facilities to do research and send reports to clients, even though he now has more and more high-tech equipment in his own home office.

POINTS FOR DISCUSSION

1. How far could it benefit you to become a teleworker?

2. Draw up a teleworking budget listing (a) the likely capital expenditure required, and (b) the likely annual costs.

3. Who do you know who is already operating as a teleworker? Ask them to tell you what they think are the main advantages and disadvantages.

6
Organising Your Office

SPOKEN FROM EXPERIENCE

'A place for everything and everything in its place.' Saying.
  'I knew it was here a minute ago.' Everyone at some time or another.
  'I like work, it fascinates me. I can sit around and look at it for hours.'
Jerome K. Jerome.

PLANNING YOUR DESK AREA

The desk is your primary work site. It pays you to run it as efficiently as
possible. This saves time, makes you more productive and stops you
becoming frustrated.

If you are right-handed the items that you use most regularly should be
to your right. This might include your contact file, a desk organiser for
pens and the phone, which can either sit on the desk or be mounted on the
wall. Wall-mounted phones have the advantage of creating more desk
space and keeping phone lines out of the way. (You could argue that the
phone should go to the left, leaving your right hand free to write with, if
you are right-handed.) A large wastepaper bin should be next to your desk
and easily accessible by your right hand.

Other items, such as calculator, printer and bookshelves should be
positioned so that most of them can be reached with just a quarter turn of
your chair and less frequently used items, still just a half turn away. This
could include the fax machine and photocopier.

Your office supplies can be given drawer space in your desk, while extra
stationery and supplies can be stored elsewhere until you need them.
Under the bed is as good a place as any. If you don't have much space
then don't over order supplies. Working on your own it takes a long time
to use up a gross of pens or ten reams of white paper.

HANDLING YOUR PAPERWORK

No matter how much you might like to think it, a mountain of jumble and
paper on your desk does not indicate the presence of a creative and

hardworking genius. It does indicate someone who is forever hunting around in a mess for information, losing pens and generally wasting time.

Often people put papers on desktops to remind them to do things. Soon the papers grow into piles and the piles begin to topple as frantic searches are made for the nugget of knowledge you know is hidden there.

If you spend ten minutes each day looking for items on your desk, by the end of the year you will have lost *one full working week* in pointless activity.

Action point
If you answer 'yes' to a lot of these questions then you may suffer from paper paralysis—a situation in which the power of paper is beginning to control you. Don't be alarmed, the condition is curable.

- Do you tend to scatter pieces of paper all over your desk?

  Yes ☐   No ☐

- Do you tell everybody not to touch a thing on your messy desk, because you know where everything is?

  Yes ☐   No ☐

- Do you leave filling in tax forms, questionnaires, applications to the last minute because you haven't organised the information you need to complete them?

  Yes ☐   No ☐

- Do you keep papers and magazines because you hope that some day you will have time to read them?

  Yes ☐   No ☐

- When you keep a piece of paper are you often unsure where to put it, and simply end up stuffing it in a drawer or cupboard?

  Yes ☐   No ☐

- Do you often misplace pieces of paper?

  Yes ☐   No ☐

How to organise your papers
There are three ways to deal with a piece of paper: respond to it, save it or bin it.

Before you think about saving a piece of paper consider what is the worst thing that can happen if you throw it away! For all but the most important documents—legal letters, bank statements and the like—the answer is nothing.

The problems involved in keeping paper are far worse. If you keep it then you will have to file it somewhere. If you haven't an appropriate filing place for it, then you have to make one which takes time and generally isn't worth the effort.

In one year Marks and Spencer eliminated one whole section of their filing system, putting 26 million stock cards and sheets of paper weighing 120 tons onto the scrap heap! There have been very few times when the decision was regretted.

Keeping excessive records shows that you are insecure. The chances are that you won't ever look again at 70-80% of the papers that you keep. So really examine the need to keep the papers you accumulate.

Continually keep a check on your filing and paper management discipline. During the day there should be no papers on your desk at all, unless you are working on them. If you haven't finished a job by the end of the day you can either gather everything into a temporary file, or keep it on the desk ready for the next day. If you do this then don't allow papers to stay there for longer than need be.

Papers that you have to act on can be divided into different categories such as To Pay, To Read, To Reply, To Follow Up, but don't make up too many categories as this only wastes time. You can use a stack of plastic letter trays to keep the paperwork efficiently sorted, but clear paper from these trays as quickly as possible. And don't set up a pending or miscellaneous file which fast becomes a dustbin for all sorts of papers.

Long-term storage

Eventually some infrequently used files will become dormant. When that happens take them out of their filing cabinets and store them away in waterproof boxes, or in boxes wrapped in plastic bags. Label the outside of the box with its contents. Purpose-built archive boxes are available which can be bought to do the job if you want to use up some money. Papers that you are legally required to keep for a fixed period of time, (VAT records for instance, have to be kept for six years) can also be stored in this way.

How to deal with letters

Letters need to be dealt with quickly and effectively. These basic rules should help you handle your correspondence without too many difficulties.

1. Sort your mail quickly. Bin items of no interest, if possible without opening them. These will generally be direct mailshots, though to the isolated worker they can provide information on interesting new products and services which you wouldn't otherwise hear about, so

sometimes give them a chance.

2. It's something of a pipe dream, but try to handle letters only once. If they need action, don't postpone that simply because of inertia. If all that's needed is to complete a simple form or similar do so immediately.

3. When you receive a letter advising of an address or phone number change, note the information in your contact file and put the letter in your rough paper box so you can use its back for notes.

4. If a letter needs a lot of research and thinking before you can answer it, schedule that action into your 'To Do' list for another day. Do not abandon today's work schedule simply to accommodate it.

5. If possible write a reply on the incoming letter and return it, keeping a photocopy for your files. This undoubtedly does save time, but really should only be done when you know the recipient, otherwise it looks as though you haven't taken any time or trouble over the reply and suggests that you're being high-handed. If you do decide to write a note in this way, soften the blow by apologising for replying in this manner and give some reason for doing so; for example shortage of time because you are just off to a meeting, but you wanted to reply by return.

6. Whatever kind of letter you are sending, come to the point quickly and be brief in your replies.

7. If you can set up a form letter on your wordprocessor, use this to reply to common requests etc.

8. If the letter you send is only for information purposes, only spend long enough on it to put your point over, and to check spelling and grammar. Don't spend ages revising it. If you intend to create a particular impression, persuade someone to do something, or to repair a bad impression, then spend as long as you need to do the job. Don't rush.

9. If possible phone rather than write. It is far quicker.

Computers and your filing

If you use a computer it is unwise to rely exclusively on its floppy disk or hard drive to keep a record of your letters, reports and other documents. At regular intervals save information to a back-up disk and onto paper. A paper copy not only is unaffected by powercuts but is often more convenient to find and look at than a computer file. If you use a typewriter you will have to make carbon copies anyway.

Consider using different coloured papers for these copies. The colours can reflect different aspects of your filing system, for instance, blue paper could be used for copies of your correspondence, yellow for notes and green for manuscripts. The different colours make it much easier to quickly pull out the necessary papers. If you file in this way then stick with the same colours.

If you use a computer, after making a hard copy of a document, write on it in which computer directory or disk you can find the original, so you know where to go instantly if you have to make a copy.

An emergency measure

Though it should never happen, if ever your desk does accumulate so many papers that you find yourself in a mess then you need to clear the overflow as fast as possible. This simple routine will quickly put you on the road to recovery.

- Stack all the papers on your desk into one large pile. Then starting at the top place each paper in one of five boxes with the following labels:

- IMPORTANT: This holds papers you *will* work on almost immediately. Each day take a paper from this box and deal with it. Build this into your daily timetable.

- URGENT: This box contains less important papers, that nevertheless still need to be done. After you finish with the important box deal with an item from here.

- IMPORTANT/NOT URGENT: At the end of the week go through this box. If you find papers that now are urgent transfer them to that box. If you come across papers that you no longer need, throw them away.

- FILE: These are papers you need to keep.

- READ: This box holds articles, leaflets and information that may be useful or entertaining. When you have finished with paper from this box either throw it away or FILE it.

Though for a time you will add new papers to the boxes, make efforts to empty each quickly. When you have emptied the boxes, resolve never to find yourself in this situation again.

HOW TO ORGANISE YOUR FILING

Whatever your type of work you will accumulate papers and documents that you need to keep, either for legal reasons or your own reference.

The complexities of your filing system will mirror the number of papers that you need to keep, but a filing system is only there to ensure that you don't lose things. It works by creating a place for every piece of paper in your office. If you can't find the papers with the right facts on them straight away then you waste time, which means you aren't earning money or moving nearer to finishing a job, but simply increasing your own stress and effort.

You do not need a complicated system that takes a lot of time to set up, or manage effectively. Indeed, the more filing you do, the more you should try to develop a filing system that is easily updated and altered. The simpler your filing system the easier it is to use.

When to start filing
Set up your filing system as soon as you can. The longer you put off the task the more papers you accumulate and the harder life becomes. And if at first your few papers seem lost in cavernous cabinets, don't worry, they will soon just be part of a crowd.

A standard filing system
You can set up a basic filing system with the minimum of equipment.

- At least one 2 or 4-drawer metal or wood filing cabinet is essential (never be tempted to keep paperwork in desk drawers, it is quickly forgotten and takes ages to sort through). These can be picked up relatively cheaply at Army Surplus stores. If your cabinet does not have rails on which suspension files can hang then you can buy metal frames which fit into the drawers and let you hang files.

- Fifty suspension files.

- Clear plastic tabs or tags to fit on the suspension files. These hold the names of each file, which are written on small pieces of card or paper.

- Fifty manilla folders, which fit inside the suspension files. As a cost-effective alternative you can recycle large (12″ × 10″) envelopes, by slitting down all but one of their long edges.

- A box of sticky labels (3½″ × 1½″).

How to create a new file
Take the papers that are to create a new file. Unfold any that are folded, remove others from their envelopes and staple together any papers that need to be kept together (paper clips do unclip).

Decide on a one or two word name for the file. This should simply be something that reminds you of the file's contents. Each file should have both a category name and a file name. For instance, if you have a client called 'XYZ Computers' you could name the file 'CLIENT - COMPUTERS, XYZ' or if you think you would remember it better then 'CLIENT - XYZ COMPUTERS'. Whatever name you decide write it on a sticky label which is then stuck on the manilla folder.

The suspension file holds the manilla folder and should never be removed from the filing cabinet drawer as it is the permanent base to which the manilla folder is always returned.

Write the name that appears on the manilla file on a piece of card which is slipped into the plastic tag on the suspension file. However, if the cabinet drawer is devoted to a single subject, for instance clients, there is no need to repeat the category name.

The plastic name tags should be put on the front edge of the suspension file, so when you run your fingers along the files to the tab you want, you automatically open the file to reveal the file inside. If you put them on the furthest edge from you when the drawer is open your fingers tend to open the file behind. You can place the name tags one behind the other so that they are flush to the right or left of the drawer, but this means that you must move the tags before you can see the tags behind. So it's probably better to stagger the name tags from left to right. Now when the drawer is opened you can immediately see the names of all the files, though every so often you need to re-position the tags as new files are added.

Do not overfill the manilla folders. This makes it more difficult to remove paper, and causes the file to rise up and hide the name tag on the suspension file. You can help matters by scoring the bottom of the suspension files so that they take on a 'U-shape' rather than a standard 'V'.

What filing system should you use?

There are three basic filing systems. You can:

- assign numbers to different files and keep track of their contents with an index. This is complicated and involves you in extra work as you will need to refer to the index before you can make any filing decisions;

- file by subject. Far easier than the above method, especially if your work covers a wide range of subjects;

- or file in alphabetic order of file names. This is the simplest system. You can develop your system further by grouping your files into categories. For example, a photographer might have a major category of 'Animals' which could be broken into three sub-files: British Animals, European Animals and American Animals. It is a mistake to create too many categories as this makes filing more difficult and time-consuming as you have to decide where a document is to go and there is a greater chance of misfiling. So at first, put all of your information on a subject in one file and when this becomes unmanageable subdivide the subject.

What types of file should you keep

Different types of information require different handling. Some need to be kept in folders, while others are more suited to storage in box files or on index cards. These are some of the basic files you might like to consider.

Tickler
One of the most important files. Use a strong concertina file with a divider numbered 1-31 for every day of the month, or Monday–Sunday when the file is only to cover a week. The jobs for each day are then filed in the appropriate sections. This can include correspondence to be answered, calls to be made, or notes to be written up. Be careful if you do use a concertina file, papers can become crumpled and trapped at the bottom of each compartment and never allow the file to become over-full.

Contacts
Contains names, addresses and telephone numbers of clients, suppliers and reference sources. This file will expand fast and you will want access to it continually. If you don't have many contacts write the names in a looseleaf address book, at least you can carry it around. Many people use index cards, one for each contact. These are filed alphabetically in index boxes, say with one box for clients and one for information sources. If you want to cross-reference with another alphabetical listing or category then pop in a cross-reference card at the time you write up the original card. If you use index cards then a rotary card file is easier to use (but more expensive) than an index box. The cards are not stacked in boxes but clipped to a horizontal spindle. As the spindle turns, new cards are brought forward and into view.

Client files
This contains information on customers for whom you have already done work. Keep these alphabetically using the client's last name. If your client generates lots of work in different areas you could subdivide their file. For example:
    Client – XYZ Computers – Invoices
    Client – XYZ Computers – Promotion & Advertising Ideas
    Client – XYZ Computers – Correspondence

Potential markets
Individuals, companies and organisations that you would like to do business with.

Business cards
Large 'wallets' are available which let you slot cards into clear plastic envelopes. However, a dedicated business card file is of dubious benefit as you have to check it in addition to your contacts file. Far better to staple the business card to a card and slot it into the appropriate place in an index card box. If you use a computer database enter the card's details and throw it away. Keep business cards only if you think the graphics or layout may help you with your own business card design.

Ideas
When you think of a good idea, write it on a card and drop it in here. Once a week review the ideas, decide which are of immediate use and which can be used in medium and long term. If the idea no longer appeals, throw it away.

Contracts
Letters of agreement and contracts are highly important documents. Make a copy of them and keep the originals separately.

Paid bills
This is a halfway house. Paid bills can either go straight into your filing system or be dropped into a Paid Bills file before passing on to your accounts system. Whichever method you choose, do your accounts regularly so that papers don't stay long in this file. Alternatively you can pay bills immediately or drop them into your tickler file to all be paid on a particular day or a series of days.

Statements/receipts
Similar to the Paid Bills file.

Clippings
Newspaper cuttings are the gremlins of the filing world. They are often small, easily crumpled, lost between other papers and quickly discolour. Date the cuttings and give their source, then stick them onto A4 sheets of scrap paper (the backs of letters you have received) and file them in large plastic wallets with zipper tops, which are labelled by category. Some people punch holes in the A4 sheets and file them in binders, but this creates extra work. If the binders are used frequently the holes soon tear and need hole reinforcers.

Correspondence
When you receive or generate a reply to a letter, staple a copy of your response to the original letter. To reduce paperwork further, carbon copy

your response onto the back of the letter you are responding to. Run this file chronologically with the most recent correspondence on top. There is generally no need to keep all your correspondence so dump covering letters and those that don't say anything.

Magazines
Special filing boxes can be bought which hold a dozen or so issues. These allow periodicals to be stacked vertically on shelves for easy access, rather than flat on the floor. It is better to go through periodicals cutting out the articles that you want and then throwing the magazines away.

Miscellaneous
Only in the most exceptional circumstances should you create misc-ellaneous files. These immediately become a dumping ground, where you put papers you haven't created a better home for. Miscellaneous files should only be used to hold temporary papers that you can either dispose of very quickly, find a new home for in the near future, or to bring together a few papers that are held in a large number of different files. Never allow many papers to accumulate in this file.

Local information
This file contains facts and figures about your local area, such as library opening and closing times, post office telephone numbers, information on secretarial services, printers or designers which you might need to look at quickly.

Hot files
These keep material that you need to check daily or things that need to be done in the very near future, off your desk but easily accessible. The hot files are hung near to your desk.

How to make a hot file
Take five or six tough, clear plastic folders, two six-feet lengths of strong cord and a cup hook. The folders should be open only at one of their long edges so either buy them like this or firmly seal the two short sides with sticky tape. Punch a couple of holes about five to six inches apart along each short side.

Pass the cord through the holes and knot it so that the cord cannot slip through the holes. Thread another folder onto the cord and again make knots in the cord. The second folder should be fixed about an inch above the first one. Do the same thing with the other folders.

Try and keep each folder parallel with the others. Now if you hold up the end of the two cords the closed long side of each folder should be nearest the floor and parallel to it. Tie the two ends of the cord together and hang the hot files near to your desk, from the cup hook. From this position it is easy to slot bits and pieces into each folder, keeping bits and pieces for different projects in sight, but out of the way.

Keep your filing flexible

If you need to file different types of material, for instance single sheets of paper together with a bulky timetable or sample, this system is very accommodating.

Begin with four or five large ring-binders. These should contain about thirty dividers, preferably with tabs. To each divider staple or stick a clear plastic folder or wallet. These plastic folders should be strong and large enough to hold quite a few bulky papers, documents or other items that can't be hole-punched. Each divider and its pocket should be used for a separate subject, or research area.

Number each divider on its tab. Don't use consecutive numbers, but in fives or tens. For example, 1, 5, 10, 15, 20 and so on. This means you can add more subjects to your folder and put the new sections near to similar subjects, without disrupting the whole system. When you have finished numbering, stick a sheet of ruled paper to the inside front cover of each binder. Use this to keep a record of the dividers' numbers and their contents. Write in pencil so you can make changes later.

Now you can store papers by hole-punching them and filing as normal, while items that can't be hole-punched are stored in the wallets. This particular system is particularly effective when developing special projects.

Filing on the floor

Some people argue that the only use for an office floor is to stop you falling on top of people below. Generally that's true. Papers stacked in corners are soon forgotten... and always topple over. For long-term storage the floor is definitely not the place.

But the floor can be used temporarily, and very successfully, for special projects. By its very nature a filing divides your paper up, but sometimes you need an overview of your material. If this is the case, spread your material out on the floor in a three-foot square. This lets you move material around. This is especially good when dealing with creative projects that require a different way of looking at them.

Using someone to do your filing

Consider employing part-time clerical help for your filing. If you are charging your time at the rate of £20-30 an hour then five hours in the week could cost you £150 of productive time. This is much more than the

£20-30 that you would have to pay for five hours of clerical help.

Bulletin boards

These need treating with care if they are not to become a magnet for paper scraps. A bulletin board can become a dustbin of all the things that you mean to do but never do. Check them once a week for redundant items and act on those you need to.

Three useful record books

Keeping track of your work is a vital part of being productive and remaining so. These are three record books that you might like to use or experiment with.

The Day Book

Buy a large, A4 sized, hard-backed book with narrow rulings. This is your Day Book. It provides a central reference point, acts as a safety net for information and stops too many individual papers creeping onto your desk.

At the start of each working day, or preferably at the end of the previous one, open the Day Book to a new double page. Date the top of the left hand page and then write down your To Do list for that day, along with the priority that you are giving each item. (To Do lists are treated in greater detail in Chapter 8, How to Organise Yourself.)

During the day this book stays open on your desk, so that you can quickly jot down notes, messages and phone conversations. The main advantage is that when you are in mid-flow you do not need to break off to look for the appropriate piece of paper to write down a note, though sometimes you will have to transfer the material over to another file later on.

The telephone log

If you make or receive many telephone calls, keep a Telephone Log, (rather than using your Day Book) in which you note down all the relevant points of your telephone conversations. This would include the time they took place, with whom, the main points of the conversation, the action you agreed on and the duration of call which is helpful if you bill clients for telephone costs.

The post book

This records when you send out letters, to whom and when you received a reply. A quick glance at your Post Book will reveal who has not replied to your letters and is due for a follow-up. It can also record postage costs which you may pass on to clients. A small, lined exercise book divided vertically into three columns is all that you need.

CASE HISTORY

When Michael set up a filing system to categorise his photographs the system worked perfectly for a few months. His photographs were categorised by subject, by location and date and client. Where necessary the photographs were cross-referenced and linked to a central card index. When a potential client phoned, Michael prided himself on being able to put his hand on any photograph quickly.

Business was very good and Michael had a hectic summer, taking on new clients and producing a lot of good photographs. But because he wasn't spending as much time as before actually in his office Michael's paperwork and photographs began to build up, and the more it accumulated, the more he put off the task of doing the filing.

Now when clients phoned up he wasn't really sure where a lot of the items were. He knew he had to knuckle down and sort the mess out, but the thought of that cross-referencing and writing out index cards just cast him into depression. After a few months, the whole system was out of control and the backlog too vast for Michael to cope with. He ended up paying a freelance secretary to come in and sort out the disaster. It took her two weeks.

Complicated filing systems may operate superbly when only a few items are involved. But in general they take longer to maintain and are more likely to break down when the pressure is on, just like Michael's. The simpler the files the less there is to go wrong.

PAPERWORK CHECKLIST

- Set aside fifteen minutes each day to do your paperwork.
- Don't put papers that you don't need on your desk.
- File papers away immediately you finish using them.
- Use a three-step paper system: To Do, To File, To Throw.
- Don't make more files than you have to.
- Don't over-complicate your filing.
- Don't put paperwork into desk drawers where it will be forgotten and lost.
- Periodically go through your filing systems and throw out paperwork you do not need.
- Test your filing system by attempting to find any piece of paper within 30-40 seconds.
- Reduce the number of papers you create by copying or printing your reply onto the backs of the letters that you receive, rather than creating another piece of paper.

7
Organising Yourself

SPOKEN FROM EXPERIENCE

'They say hard work never hurt anybody, but I figured why take the chance.' Ronald Reagan, one-time actor and some-time President.

'You know what the trouble with peace is? No organisation.' Bertold Brecht, playwright, from *Mother Courage*.

'The best motivation you can have in improving the organisation of your life and work is... laziness and a love of freedom.' Lennart Meynert, time management expert.

'Time is the stuff of which life is made.' Benjamin Franklin.

'If I had to sum up in one word the qualities that make a good manager, I'd say it all comes down to decisiveness... in the end you have to bring all of your information together, set up a timetable, and act.' Lee Iacocca, American car executive.

YOUR TIME IS VALUABLE

No matter what your business, or how long you spend in your home office, the proper organisation of your office and work methods is vital if you are going to be as effective a homeworker as possible and produce the best work you can.

Some homeworkers claim that the potential for 'chaotic informality' at home helps them work better. They say this gives the freedom to be instinctive about the way they run their business. This relaxed type of approach may suit you, but for most people it is a chaotic recipe.

When you work from home, you operate in a highly informal environment, and if you are not careful then this informality can slip into your working life. When that happens you become less productive, waste time and lose money. Worse still you may not immediately realise what has happened until it is almost too late.

Most homeworkers discover that to work effectively they must create a 'formal' structure similar to that found in a traditional office. This offers protection from the temptations and disruptions of the day that can waste

93

so much time... and wasting time can be expensive, very expensive.

The cost of wasting your time

When you waste time during the working day you pour money down the drain. A few simple sums illustrate the point. This table shows hourly pay rates for a variety of incomes. It assumes you work forty hours for forty-eight weeks in the year.

Income	Hourly rate	Minute rate	Cost of 15 minutes lost each day for a year
£10,000	£5.20	8.6p	£309.60
£15,000	£7.81	13.0p	£468.00
£20,000	£10.41	17.3p	£622.80
£25,000	£13.02	21.7p	£781.20
£30,000	£15.62	26.0p	£936.00

In reality these rates apply only if you work for someone else who pays your salary or wage. If you are a self-employed homeworker these hourly rates should be higher. This is because while you may be working forty hours a week, you may only be earning for twenty-five of them. After all, there are bound to be times when you don't have the work or have to do administration which doesn't earn a penny, but only costs you time. If you were only earning for twenty-five hours a week, your hourly rate would rise to £25 and the time lost over the year would leap to £1,500!

Calculating your non-productive time in this way not only makes you value the cost of wasted time, but also helps you in setting a proper charge for your services. Looked at in these terms your day rate may be hopelessly inadequate if you are only going to be earning money three-quarters of the time.

Action point

Work out an hourly rate for your own services. Try and assess just how many hours a week will be money earning ones and not just eaten up in administration or paper pushing.

How do you waste time?

You probably say that you don't have the time to do all of the things that you want or need to do. But in general this is not the real reason that stops you from completing, or even starting jobs. Even if you gave some people as much time as they wanted to do a job, through some strange quirk they still wouldn't have enough time to finish it.

None of us can use all of our time to best effect, but the less we waste the more we achieve. These are some of the most likely reasons why time is wasted.

Action Point 1

If you answer 'yes' to most of these questions, you probably waste a lot of your time.

- Do you constantly hunt through papers for information you know is there... somewhere?
  Yes ☐   No ☐

- Do you tend to gossip on the phone?
  Yes ☐   No ☐

- Do you think you take too many coffee breaks in the day?
  Yes ☐   No ☐

- Do you read magazine articles when you should be working?
  Yes ☐   No ☐

- Do you try to do too many things at once rather than just one?
  Yes ☐   No ☐

- Do you put off doing things that you need to do?
  Yes ☐   No ☐

- Do you become distracted by trivial things?
  Yes ☐   No ☐

- Do you make up reasons to go out rather than stay at your desk?
  Yes ☐   No ☐

List six more ways in which you regularly waste time. These can be a combination of large and small. Write them in the spaces below.

Action Point 2

List six things that regularly distract you from what you are doing. Alongside each write down a substitute activity for that distraction. These replacement items should take no longer than five minutes to complete.

For instance, if you are always nipping off to make a sandwich, then every time this urge comes upon you engage in your 'better' substitute activity. This could be ten sit-ups, eating an apple or doing relaxation exercises. Though it would be better if you weren't distracted at all, these little acts of self-discipline are not only good for you, but can stop you becoming an overweight slouch. Pin this list up near to your desk where you can see it.

THE ADVANTAGES OF PLANNING

By carefully planning your work life then you have more time to do the things that you want to do, such as spending more time with your family, taking flying lessons, or walking the dog.

When you plan your day, because you know in advance what you are going to do throughout the day, you don't constantly have to make decisions about what to do next. This reduces your stress load, improves your temper and saves you time. The time you will take to plan your day, is far less than the time you lose by not doing it.

TIME MANAGEMENT TECHNIQUES

When do you work best?

You probably have a fair idea whether you are a lark or an owl. But if you don't, for five consecutive working days, complete the Sleep/Alertness Table shown here. To do this, in the middle of every two hour period eg. 7am, 11am, 5pm, simply circle the number that is closest to the way you feel. So if you feel pretty sleepy at seven o'clock in the morning circle 4, if you feel very alert circle 1.

	Sleep/Alertness Table							
	6-8	8-10	10-12	12-2	2-4	4-6	6-8	8-10
1. Alert & energetic	1	1	1	1	1	1	1	1
2. Alert, not quite at peak	2	2	2	2	2	2	2	2
3. Awake but not fully alert	3	3	3	3	3	3	3	3
4. A bit slow, relaxed	4	4	4	4	4	4	4	4

At the end of the five days you should see a pattern emerging with either a lot of 1s and 2s in the morning (with 3s and 4s in the afternoon), if you are at your best in the morning and the reverse if you are better in the afternoon and evening. However, a fairly even spread of numbers means that you are neither a lark nor an owl.

With this information you can manage and plan your working day to better and greater effect, performing those tasks that need your greatest concentration when you are at your most alert, and saving mundane tasks for your 'flatter' periods.

Ideally you should be able to mould the day as you want to, but family and other commitments put limitations on your time. For instance, you may have to take and pick up the children from school. This means that you can never work between 8.30 and 9 am or between 3.30 and 4.00. Try to work out in advance what commitments will cut into your day, note the times down and work around them.

General rule
The more you achieve first thing in the morning the better. Then if the worst does come to the worst and the pipes burst later on you will have achieved something.

Using lists
Writing lists is one of the best ways of ensuring you complete tasks on time. A list provides you with definite evidence of what you must do and makes you feel guilty when you don't do it. Once a task is written down you make a commitment to do it and can't then conveniently forget about it.

- Before the beginning of each working day and preferably the night before, make a list of the jobs you must do. This can include tasks for that day, the next day or the week ahead. Include a few simple and quick tasks because completing these gives you a psychological boost because you feel you are moving forward. This is particularly important if you are involved in a larger project. This is your Master List which can be kept in your Day Book (see Chapter 7).

- Some time management experts recommend that you use ABC priority lists. The 'A' list holds the most important items that you have to do, the 'B' list less important jobs and the 'C' list is made up of bottom-of-the-pile jobs.

- For longer term jobs make another list. However, include on your Master List at least one element from each of those long-term jobs that you can achieve in the week. For instance, if you want to produce a brochure for a trade exhibition in four months' time, 'Create Brochure' goes on your Long-Term List, while on your

Master List you write 'Organise Photographs for Brochure', which reminds you to speak to a photographer during the week and so keep the project moving along.

- Any jobs left on the list at the end of the day should be transferred to the next day's list. However, be careful. If items are constantly transferred you are putting off doing them. Find out why. If need be use some of the anti-procrastination techniques described in Chapter 9 on problem solving.

- Once you have chosen to do something then the next step is simply to do it.

Setting priorities

If you confuse the urgent with the important you aren't using your time productively. Organisational expert Edwin C Bliss says that all tasks can be put into one of five categories.

The important and the urgent
These jobs have to be done very soon. They take priority over everything else and therefore cause no real problems.

The important but not urgent
Even though they are important these tasks will be postponed forever if you let them. Into this area will fall your long-term goals and plans such as taking a business skills seminar or writing a new promotional brochure that sells your business better.

The urgent but not important
Low priority they may be but these jobs always seem to be jumping up in front of us shouting 'I'm next, I'm next.' And because they are so 'noisy' we tend to do them before more important but less urgent jobs.

Busy work
These jobs let us off the hook. They are just about worth doing and so we do them to put off tackling harder tasks.

Wasted time
Only you can decide which jobs really aren't worth doing at all.

Action point

From today begin to prioritise all your activities in this way. Try and get as many Important but not Urgent jobs onto your Master List as possible.

Developing a daily schedule

Without the rigid structure of the traditional workplace, many distractions can shape the homeworker's day in altogether undesirable ways if given half a chance.

To counter this you must create your own daily schedule just as though you were an employer setting the workload for one of the staff. In this way you create signposts in your day which point the direction forward rather than letting you wander along aimlessly.

Because work really does expand to fill the time available for it, the more you have to do in the day, the more you will get done. You should therefore try and plan every minute and each hour in the work days that stretch ahead.

At the end of each day spend fifteen minutes planning in detail what you are going to do the next day, and more broadly what you are going to do over the next few weeks.

Your daily schedule should balance work, rest and free time so that you maximise productivity whilst minimising stress and time wasting.

Making up a personal timetable

On a sheet of A4, or recycled mail, draw up a grid similar to the one shown. On the left side fill in the time periods that you are going to work within. These could be 30, 45, 50 minutes. It is hard to concentrate for much longer than this in any case.

There is no reason why you should work to the same length of time slot throughout the day. If you find that you can concentrate for longer periods in the morning but tire in the afternoon then work to fifty-minute periods in the morning and thirty minutes in the afternoon.

Include ten or fifteen-minute breaks at the end of each work period. Time some of these breaks for 'natural' breaks in the day, say when the children come home, or the postman arrives. Then you won't be trying to work through disruptions and distractions. Also arrange a thirty to sixty-minute break around lunch time or early evening if you habitually work late.

However, for tasks requiring a long time to become absorbed it's preferable to work for longer periods, rather than having to keep on warming up after frequent breaks. If this is the case still take thirty to sixty-second breaks to give you a temporary respite.

Using the items on your Master List begin filling in the time slots. You do not need to be too specific when writing down the tasks. A simple 'write letter to bank', 'ideas for tourist project', or 'start computer projection' is enough.

Try and do the hardest or most complicated tasks when your mind is fresh early in the day and leave the routine and mundane jobs as far as possible for later in the day.

Once you have planned your day, try to stick to this routine, but don't be a slave to it. It is worthwhile building in some buffer time, perhaps by breaking off from a task five or ten minutes early, or over-budgeting the time for a job. Then if your day becomes ten or fifteen minutes 'out of synch' you can catch up. However, if business dictates it, be prepared to change your planned day.

Some people may not like to create such a rigid structure and of course it is up to you whether you follow your timetable to the minute. However, it does provide a strong foundation for the day and you should not be too quick to dismiss the services of this substitute boss and taskmaster.

Of course meetings and interviews will throw the structure of your normal timetable out of the window, so simply pick up your schedule at a convenient point.

When you have become 'grooved' in your standard working day you may find it easier to photocopy your daily timetables rather than draw all the time slots every day.

As a check on productivity, periodically compare the amount of work you are actually achieving in your day against what your timetable says you planned to achieve.

Case history – June plans her day
Figure 4 is an example of a daily schedule that Jane, a freelance journalist, created for herself. Of the ten hours between 8am and 6pm she intends to work seven hours. Because she has planned her day and breaks it up so as to give herself a break from specific tasks she accomplishes a great deal.

Stop being a mail addict
Working from home means you hear the postman arrive, which can be a great distraction, so stifle the urge to shoot off and find what he or she has brought you. Not only does fetching the mail take time, but once you start opening or reading it, then fifteen minutes can easily be lost, and the rhythm of a work session is broken.

There is nothing that won't wait for another twenty or thirty minutes. Rather, wait until one of your breaks and then take a look. Tell others in the house not to bring in the mail to you.

If you generally cannot contain your excitement at the postman's arrival and can't concentrate until you have read and inwardly digested everything that has dropped through your letterbox, then you must build this interruption into your daily schedule.

One possibility is to start work well before the postman regularly arrives. Then because you have already done sixty minutes or so of work before he arrives you can succumb to your mail addiction without

TIMETABLE		DATE ....
Start/finish	Activity	Time Spent (minutes)
8.00 - 8.50	Write car article, 1st draft	50
8.50 - 8.55	Coffee break & check post	5
8.55 - 9.45	Write car article (cont)	50
9.45 - 9.55	Phone bank	10
9.55 - 10.45	Make notes for business article	50
10.45 - 10.55	Chase unpaid invoice	10
10.55 - 11.40	Gather names for mailshot	45
11.40 - 12.00	Visit post office	20
12.00 - 12.45	Write up two new article ideas	45
12.45 - 1.45	Lunch	
1.45 - 2.30	Edit business article, 2nd draft	45
2.30 - 2.40	Organise future interview	10
2.40 - 3.20	Conduct phone interview	40
3.20 - 3.30	Coffee	
3.30 - 4.10	Finish business article	40
4.10 - 4.25	Take walk in garden	
4.25 - 5.05	Telephone research/animal story	40
5.05 - 5.15	Coffee	
5.15 - 6.00	Finish business article	45

Fig. 4. A sample daily schedule.

breaking a work session or feeling guilty.

As far as possible set an allotted time for dealing with your mail and stick to it. If you do not have much mail, deal with it all at once. If you have a mountain of it or complicated correspondence, then deal with the urgent material at once and set aside the rest to be dealt with later in the day.

Using breaks to advantage

Rather than just using your break to rest, you can positively fill it with a change in activity that is either personal (knitting or drawing) or work related (a switch to filing or writing a letter). Select an activity that easily fits into these few minutes. Do not choose something that could cause you to overrun your break because it is too absorbing. Reading a novel or cooking would come into this category, as you would have to stop and go back to work before you had to finish or 'get into' it.

- Don't wait until you are tired before having a break. Take frequent thirty-second intervals when you lift up your head from work, have a stretch and relax your eyes. As a matter of routine have a five-minute 'pause' every forty-five minutes or so.

If you are particularly tired then take even longer breaks. Don't feel guilty about doing this. You will be more effective afterwards, working faster and making fewer mistakes.

However, be fair to yourself. You must be your own manager. If you get up from your seat as soon as the going gets tough, saying that you need a break, then you will never achieve anything.

Plan these breaks into your day's timetable, and don't be ashamed about taking them. This is one of the perks of working from home, you really can shape your day in a way that others can't. Let them envy you.

Case history – Diana's personal goals

Diana is an independent producer of television programmes. As well as her business objectives, she has two personal ambitions for the year. She wants to become fitter and also learn Italian.

Because Diana is not able to allocate large amounts of time to exercise or language learning, she incorporates them into her work breaks. During three of her daily ten-minute breaks she does sit-ups, press-ups and stretching exercises. In her eighty-minute lunch break she works out to an aerobics tape, then showers and makes a light lunch.

In three other fifteen-minute breaks, Diana improves her Italian, reading books and listening to cassettes. Diana has also set herself a long-term reward—an Italian holiday at the end of year, but only if her Italian is good enough!

Action point
Make a list of twenty different activities which you can slot into your
breaks. These should take between five and thirty minutes to complete.

How to change your bad habits
Misusing your time is generally the result of a well established pattern of
behaviour, not just an occasional event. You can use your breaks to help
end a bad habit. Do this by rewarding yourself for completing a
complicated job or making a difficult call with a small treat. This is called
reinforcing behaviour.

All of the following could be rewards:

Eating a piece of fruit	Drinking a coffee
Eating a chocolate bar	Going for a walk
Buying something new	Going to the pub that evening
Listening to a favourite record	Having an extra long soak in the bath

Action point
Make a list of twenty potential rewards. Make some of these small and
some large, such as taking a holiday.

How to improve your concentration
Self-discipline is something of a lost art. It is one that you must rediscover
if you are going to work successfully from home. The more uninterrupted
time you can spend on a task the faster and more effectively you will do it.
Working in 'bits of time' is not so effective.

- To help you concentrate solely on the task in hand minimise sources
  of potential disruption. Use your telephone answering machine to
  screen calls or just record messages so that you can get down to the
  business of completing work undisturbed. You must still be tough
  on yourself, it is easy to pick up the receiver if you hear a friend
  asking you out for lunch. Turn down the volume and don't be
  tempted.

- If you do answer a telephone call at an inconvenient time, tell the
  caller that you will call back at a more convenient time. But reassure
  your caller that you will call back at a specific time and stick to your
  promise. If you won't be able to make the call then phone and say
  you will phone at another specific time.

Callers who want to socialise on the telephone can eat into your
precious time. Set the whole tone of the call by adopting a business-like
voice that suggests you have no time for chit-chat.

- If you use an electric typewriter, keep it switched on. The sound of it humming away can be a terrific spur to completing a typing project. The buzz cuts through the silence, making you feel guilty that the machine is idle.

- According to Japanese research, smells of lemon and eucalyptus are said to improve the concentration, for instance reducing keyboard errors by over 50%. Try it, it may work for you too.

Example

The tale is told of Thomas Carlyle, the nineteenth-century author of a book on the French Revolution who gave the manuscript to his friend, John Stuart Mill, for proofreading. Mill's housemaid, not knowing what she was doing, took the papers and used them to light a fire. Suppressing the natural emotion to just give the whole thing up as a bad job, Carlyle sat down and wrote the book again, without the aid of notes, or the tremendous advantages of a wordprocessor. That is not only an act of great concentration but determination.

Set yourself objectives

Don't be aimless in your work. Try to set objectives for every area, whether that is filing, selling, writing, or general planning.

- Make your objectives tangible and specific. You will call ten people in the next hour. You will complete all your filing by eleven o'clock.

- Make your objectives realistic but challenging.

- Use your Master List and your Daily Schedule to fit these objectives into your working day, week or month.

- Remind yourself continually of your longer term objectives. Write down on an index card some of the goals you want to achieve, but for one reason or another tend to ignore. Don't write down obvious goals—rather those that you would not do without being reminded about. These goals might be to start a book, learn better sales skills, or improve your computer knowledge. Keep the card with you and look at it frequently. The more you do this, the less intimidating these tasks become. When you think of new ideas add them to the card, but limit the list to six or seven items. Make sure that you are listing objectives or goals, not specific jobs. Now do something each week to achieve your goals.

Set deadlines for yourself

In the traditional office you are in a race to complete your work before the boss tells you off, before a colleague finishes a similar piece of work and gets the praise not you, and against the train which never leaves on time except when you work late.

The homeworker has none of these spurs to finish work quickly and so must replace them with their own personal competitions:

- Use a deadline as a friend not an enemy. Set deadlines for each task that you have to do. Tell yourself that you will finish this letter before three o'clock. But don't be incredibly hard on yourself if you miss it. That is negative.

- Pin your longer term deadlines on the wall near your desk where you will see them constantly.

- Tell friends and family about your deadlines and encourage them to hound you on your progress. With this extra encouragement you soon make sure that work is done if you continually have to admit you are missing targets.

- Compete against the clock. Buy a simple clockwork timer. Break your current task into convenient blocks, then set your timer for thirty or forty-five minutes, and try to finish the task before the bell rings. This is long enough to constructively achieve something but within the limits of your concentration.

The balance method of decision taking
Two centuries ago, Benjamin Franklin devised a simple, but highly effective method of decision making. Take a sheet of paper and divide it into two columns. Write 'FOR' above the left column and 'AGAINST' above the right. Now, when faced with a decision write down all of the factors involved in making it. Some of these will be 'cons' and others 'pros'. When you have written down all of these, one side will outweigh the other in the number of factors it has. Make your decision accordingly.

Ideas to keep you motivated and working
Always be on the look out for new ways to motivate yourself as some of your favourite tricks may inexplicably stop working for you. So it is good to have others up your sleeve.

- As soon as you have a job to do, take the first steps to ensuring its completion. Pin up a completed invoice for the job in front of you. By doing this you make a commitment to the job.

- Make use of small signs or large stickers in your work-place. Two that really hit home when you are slacking are: 'Do it now', or 'Some people make things happen, some people watch things happen, some people say—What happened?' It's known as creating a Positive Mental Attitude.

- Don't leave a magazine on your desk otherwise the devil will tempt you away from the jobs that you really need to do. Put magazines and newspapers on one side. Read them during one of your breaks.

- Don't think that there is only one way to do a job. Don't waste time waiting for the perfect way to pop into your head, get stuck in.

- If you have to do something that will interrupt the usual flow of the day, such as having to make a telephone call at a particular time, then make a note to do just that on a small red index card. Keep this on your desk. It acts as a vivid reminder of what you must do.

- Always ask yourself, how can I best use my time right now? Is what I am doing moving me forward, or am I being sidetracked?

- Your subconscious ensures that you think your best thoughts at the most inconvenient times so always carry a notebook around with you. Whenever you think of something concerning your business or life in general jot it down. You can develop the idea later. Never rely on your memory no matter how magnificent you rate it. It only takes one brilliant idea to be lost out of a hundred other thoughts to have you gnashing teeth.

ASSESSING YOUR PRODUCTIVITY

When you work from home it is important to keep a check on your productivity, gauging your current performance and seeing if you are making improvements.

The time log
This is a most useful tool that can be used when you first start working from home and for periodic assessments of your work rate.

Divide a sheet of paper into four colums as shown in Figure 5. Above the left column on the far left write 'Start', above the column next to it write 'Finish'. Above the wide centre column write 'Activity' and above the column on the right put 'Time spent'.

Tape the time log to your desk close to where you work. Write the times you start and finish each new task on the time log. At the end of the day your list of activities should include all the interruptions such as telephone calls and wasteful activities, such as hunting for a file.

Don't be surprised if the total only comes to four, five or six hours. A productive five-hour day working from home can achieve the same results as a working day twice that long at a conventional office.

From your time log you can work out how much time you are spending doing different tasks. At first keeping a time log will seem like an irritating waste of time, but very soon you will fall into a rhythm. Don't keep your

Time Log

Started	Finished	Activity	Total (mins)
8.05	8.25	Letter writing	20
8.25	8.30	Phone call	5
8.30	8.45	Take kids to school	15
8.45	8.55	Coffee	10
8.55	9.00	Check mail	5
9.00	9.15	Talk with wife	15
9.15	9.45	Letter writing	30
9.45	10.10	Phone call from client	25
10.10	10.20	Coffee	10
10.20	10.30	Read awhile in paper	10
10.30	10.55	Filing	25
10.55	11.00	Interruption by wife	5
11.00	11.05	Call to garage about car	5
11.05	11.40	Print out report	35
11.40	11.55	Call from parents	15
11.55	12.10	Coffee	15
12.10	12.25	Call from accountant	15
12.25	12.30	Interruption by wife	5
12.30	1.00	Design brochure logo	30
1.00	2.00	Lunch	60
2.00	2.15	Read paper	15

Fig. 5. Example of a time log used by a freelance public
relations consultant. The log shows that too many interruptions
are breaking up the day and affecting productivity.

time log for more than a few days at a time, a week at the most. This gives
you enough time to see where you are spending your time.

Often you will see that your memory really has been playing you false—
on apparently highly busy days you really have only been productive for a
small part of the time. Never cheat on your time log to make yourself feel
better. It is a tool for you to learn from.

The Time Progress (TIP) Sheet

When you work on projects for clients, or for yourself, it is important to
keep careful track of the time you spend on different aspects of the job.
This gives an indication if the project is becoming unbalanced with too
much time being spent on one area. The Time Progress Sheet also allows
you to accurately work out your expenses.

The TIP Sheet (see Fig. 6) is for a writer and journalist. This shows the
length of time that each part of the job is expected to take and an actual
running total of the time spent. If this starts to grow much larger than the
expected time, you should consider reassessing the project. You can
design a TIP sheet that is best suited to your individual work pattern.

How to use a situation summary

At the end of each day, week, month and year, you should undertake a
summary of your situation. This helps you identify potential problems
and clarify your mind.

Daily and weekly summaries

At the end of each day or week, write a quick summary of what you have
achieved during that time. Be honest with yourself. If the day hasn't gone
well identify the reasons. Were there unavoidable interruptions, were you
under the weather, did you just have a lazy day, did you put off jobs that
you should have done today? What can you do to stop this happening
again? Can you push the interruptions to another less troublesome time?

These short-term summaries are useful in keeping you moving along
the right track and at the right pace. They give you an early warning of
when you are consistently falling behind with your work.

Monthly and yearly summaries

The summaries that you undertake at the end of each month and year are
more thorough affairs that can also provide the basis for a marketing
document, or business plan that can be presented to accountants or bank
managers.

While daily and weekly summaries can be just mental, longer term
summaries should be written down in detail. They are important
procedures for you and should deal only in specifics, not wishful

```
┌─────────────────────────────────────────────────────────────┐
│                                                               │
│                    TIME PROGRESS SHEET                        │
│                                                               │
│   Client:_____    │
│   Job:_____     │
│   Title/subject:_____     │
│   Deadline date:_____     │
│   Agreed fee:_____     │
│                                                               │
│                                                               │
│   TIME REQUIRED              EXPECTED                         │
│   ACTUAL                                                      │
│   Briefing:_____     │
│   Library research:_____     │
│   Telephone research:_____     │
│   Research travel time:_____     │
│                                                               │
│                                                               │
│   Organisation of material:_____     │
│   Writing time:_____     │
│   Rewrite time:_____     │
│   Proofreading:_____     │
│                                                               │
│                                                               │
│   Additional needs:_____     │
│   Design time:_____     │
│   Photographic session time:_____     │
│   Packaging:_____     │
│   Total time required for job:_____     │
│   Income per hour:_____     │
│                                                               │
└─────────────────────────────────────────────────────────────┘
```

Fig. 6. Example of a time progress sheet.

thinking. They should include the following information:

- *The problem as you see it:* This should clearly state what your present circumstances are, identifying any problems and describing them in a couple of sentences.

- *What are you going to do about your situation?* You need to be specific in the steps that you are going to take. Include the dates that you hope to achieve your targets and what resources you need to achieve these goals.

- *How are you going to benefit from taking these steps?* What are the benefits to you in terms of extra income, quality of service, flexibility, the freeing of extra time and improvement in work conditions?

- *How much is taking these steps going to cost?* You will need to work this out in terms of both time and money.

- *Other courses of action:* What else can you do to achieve your goals? List other options in order of preference. What is the best reason for *not* taking that particular course of action?

- *Who can help you?* Who are the people who can help you achieve your goals. Make a list of them and decide how to approach them and for what purpose.

- *Set a review date.* This will be the day on which you look at your situation summary again and look to see what has changed or how well you are progressing in hitting your targets. On this date assess how close you are to achieving your goals within the time limits you have set yourself. If you haven't hit your targets, why haven't you?

More time saving measures
- If you haven't created a 'to go' area then make sure that you don't forget things when heading for a meeting, by putting them in the doorway of the office.

- Keep personal calls as treats and make them during your breaks. Put a sticky label on your coffee cup to remind you.

- If you find methods of saving yourself time or making yourself more efficient then stick with it, no matter how bizarre or odd it may seem to others.

8
Overcoming Problems

SPOKEN FROM EXPERIENCE

'While people do not mind change, they do mind being changed.' D L Foster.

'A problem left to itself dries up or goes rotten. But fertilise a problem with a solution—you'll hatch dozens.' N F Simpson.

'It is quite a three-pipe problem.' Sherlock Holmes.

'A problem shared is a problem halved.' Old saying.

'Many of us spend half our time wishing for things we could have if we didn't spend half our time wishing.' Alexander Woollcott.

PROBLEMS OF WORKING FROM HOME

No matter how much you would like it to, working from home does not solve all of life's problems. Indeed it can bring its own set of problems. No matter how well you run your home business, problems will arise.

It is easy to let difficulties develop into Himalayan proportions when working in the glorious isolation of home especially as you have no colleagues around who can shoulder some of the burden, or boost your morale. And since home and office cannot be separated, a business problem cannot be physically left behind. It lurks not very far away, up the stairs, in the spare bedroom or down in the kitchen.

The most common homeworking problems fall into three categories:

- the problems of loneliness
- the problems caused by your family and neighbours
- the problems that you cause yourself.

Some of these will not rear their ugly heads for a year or two, but some will materialise much sooner.

HANDLING LONELINESS

The traditional office offers great opportunities for meeting people. There

111

you can chat, gossip and generally plug yourself into the world. When you work from home all that disappears. For some homeworkers, this brings a great feeling of isolation. Such loneliness can be highly demoralising and stressful.

But any homeworker who wants to be successful must counter these feelings. For those content with their own company, this is relatively easy, however for the extrovert or the insecure it can become all too much, forcing them very quickly to seek a return to the security of the busy, noisy outside world of others that not long before they were so keen to leave.

How to overcome loneliness
If you think you will suffer greatly from loneliness, then it is vital to build a time for social contact into your day to convince you that there is a world beyond the four walls of your office.

So try and get out into the real world, if not once a day then at least a couple of times each week. Do not feel guilty about building this into your schedule. You are not playing truant. Just regard this as a means of keeping your sanity and making you more productive. You would be doing this anyway if you were working in a conventional manner, so do it when you are working from home.

Take a walk to the shops, a stroll in the fields or a drive in the car. There is no need for you 'to do' something with this time, though you can if you wish. But be careful not to abuse this social time.

Unless there is a very good reason not to, set a time for starting back to work and stick to it, otherwise you can end up chatting with a friend you meet and extend your break by half an hour or more.

Music and the radio can be a great way of staying in touch and provides companionship. Whether you listen to Radio 1, Radio 4 or classical music is up to you, as long as you are not too distracted. If you have a task to do that needs concentration, listen to soothing music rather than a talk show.

Create your own network of homeworkers
There is a great benefit in using your fellow homeworkers to help banish loneliness. They are all too aware of the isolation you may be feeling. Meeting and talking with them reminds you that you aren't alone. Why not make a regular commitment to meet them and talk over your day, your future plans or any problems that you may be having? Like-minded professionals can provide much needed boosts of morale, ideas and contacts. As well as being a mutual support group, such a network can also act as a magnet for business. A heavy workload that can't be handled by one homeworker can be subcontracted to another member of the network.

An informal network can even pool its resources and talents to go after contracts than would otherwise be too large or complicated for just one of its members. If organised professionally, your network can offer virtually the same services of a much larger company, but at much lower cost and with additional credibility.

In the early days of your homeworking career, you can also try bartering with other members of your network, offering your services or goods for theirs. For instance, a graphic designer could produce some artwork for a photographer's brochure, while the photographer provides pictures for the designer's. This can be a valuable cost-cutting option when money is tight.

Action point
In the space below, make a list of the people who can help you and who you can help. Make a point of discovering their phone numbers. This will form the basis of your network.

Name   *How they can help*   *Phone number*

_____

_____

_____

_____

OVERCOMING LACK OF CONFIDENCE

New homeworkers often lack confidence in what they are doing. After years spent commuting into town there seems to be something not quite right about staying at home all day.

This can be especially difficult for men who traditionally are the ones who 'go out' to work each day. By staying at home all day they often feel they have gone down in the eyes of the world. Women tend to suffer less from this blow to self esteem, because their work is still seen by some to be in the home anyway. Neighbours and friends often make the situation worse with jibes about 'when are you going to find a proper job?'. This only serves to reinforce any uneasiness a homeworker can feel about what they are doing.

Are you taking homework seriously?
If you lack confidence about working from home, then you must first identify what is causing the problem.

- Do you feel that you cannot do the job, because you are too inexperienced or need the help of others? If so, this probably means you are uncertain about getting work in the first place and then completing it to the client's satisfaction. Or are you just being modest about your talents? If you aren't what can you do about acquiring the skills you need?

- Do you subconsciously see working from home as a soft option? If you do, then you will fritter away your work time because there are so many pleasant distractions around to pull you away from the nasty business of work.

- Do your family, friends and neighbours fail to take you seriously because it looks as though you are playing at work and not taking yourself seriously?

How to be more positive when working from home
Make sure that family, friends and neighbours know that just because you are at home does not mean that you aren't working. Get them on your side—tell them not to call up for chats on the phone or to make visits of the 'I just thought I'd drop by as you're at home' variety. Tell them that you work between certain hours and would appreciate them not coming round or phoning. Explain that between these times you are just not available. Even if you don't work during these hours they won't know that.

- Develop the appearance and attitudes of a professional as quickly as possible. Feeling professional and doing things professionally makes you feel confident and confidence makes you work harder and better.

- Leave your answer machine on so that you can screen calls. If friends can't reach you for a chat, they will eventually look for more fertile conversational pastures.

MANAGING FAMILY AND FRIENDS

Do not think you have no need for people skills when you work from home. It's true you won't have to deal with a grumpy boss or unruly subordinates, but you still have to deal with suppliers, clients, unwanted phone calls, members of your family, pets, friends, neighbours, blocked drains and the washing up. All of these play their part in throwing spanners into the carefully organised routine of your day. Interruptions are a fact of life, but you can take positive steps to keep them under control.

How to deal with the family

When someone begins to work from home, it changes the whole pattern of domestic and family life. Instead of being away from home all day, they are now at home all day. This naturally disrupts the particular rhythm which every family builds up over the years and feels comfortable with. If that rhythm is affected too much then there will be quarrels, disagreements and difficulties that will make the homeworker far less effective.

There are four main reasons why people will be negative about you working from home:

- through sheer habit they are comfortable with the old ways.

- they misunderstand what you are trying to do and what home-working is.

- they feel left out of your work.

- they feel threatened because they don't know what changes will need to be made so that you can work from home.

For instance, some family members will be highly negative about the whole business, deriding your efforts at every turn. Comments such as 'if you are going to be at home all day, then why can't you do this?', or 'this will only take a minute to do' indicate that the family has not come to terms with you being home and just do not recognise the fact that you are working. There is the subconscious assumption that you are somehow playing at work.

For female homeworkers there is often the additional strain of being expected to still run the household without help—a difficult enough proposition especially when young children are involved.

But don't think that any problems that arise will all be the fault of others. It is very easy to expect far too much of your non-homeworking wife or husband. You must remember that though your work is important to the family and that home is where you now work, you cannot expect the rest of the family to turn their lives upside down to satisfy your demands.

Some homeworkers become rather precious about their work and refuse to do household chores if they come at the wrong time. If you demand that the rest of the family protects you from the world, there is bound to be a simmering resentment if you are seen to do all of the taking and none of the giving... and soon.

Dealing with babies and children

Whenever possible make your office an accessible place for your children. Perhaps they can come in when you are doing menial chores that do not need much of your attention?

- Make certain that you will schedule time into your day when you will play with the children or read to them.

- Make at least part of the week a work-free time when the family know that you will definitely be with them. For instance, this could be Sunday lunch.

- If you do have to reprimand the children for being noisy when you are on the phone, explain why what they have done has caused a problem. Be specific.

Hiring child care

Many parents find it impossible to look after children and work at the same time. Instead, they either use a nursery or employ a child-minder so that their offspring aren't neglected or do not cause a nuisance when mummy or daddy is at work. Hiring such care when you are at home yourself may seem an extravagance, however it can be anything but. Imagine that to fit in with the demands of your children you could only work from nine-to-twelve and then again from two-to-four, that gives you the potential for a five-hour working day. However, eating into that, is time spent comforting crying children, making their meals, and sorting out squabbles. All of these distractions could take another hour off your day, by the time you have settled back to work.

On the other hand, if you hired a nanny you might be able to lengthen your work hours to seven a day, say nine-to-five with an hour for lunch. And without the distractions, that is solid time spent working. So if you cost your time at £10 an hour, then as long as your nanny isn't costing more than £30 a day, you are better off hiring the help.

Most homeworkers interested in hiring child care help will look at employing either a child-minder or a nanny. Child-minders work from their own homes, set their own hours, expect you to bring your children to them and will generally look after several other children at the same time. Make sure that the child-minder is registered with the local authorities and preferably use one that is recommended by a trusted friend. In any case inspect their home before sending your child along. Your local authority's Social Services Department will hold a list of registered child-minders.

Nannies, on the other hand, work for you, to your hours and in the way that you want. When interviewing a nanny ask them about the kinds of routine that they have been taught to use. If this is too different from your own child care regime, you may have difficulties. But never expect a nanny to agree with you in every detail, no-one will bring up your child quite like you do.

If the cost of a nanny seems too high, you might be able to halve the cost by sharing her with a (homeworking) neighbour.

You should set up your system of child care well before you need to. Then you can accustom your child to the new situation and if there are problems sort them out before they grow too large.

Case history – A mother of three

Ann has three children, the oldest just six years old. 'I work from home because it gives me the flexibility I need,' she says. 'I just couldn't do a nine-to-five job with three children in tow.'

On average, Ann works thirty hours each week. While the oldest child goes to school, a nanny comes in from nine-to-three to look after the other two, 'though to begin with I shared a nanny with another homeworker so we could halve the cost,' says Ann. 'Now that I'm earning more money that doesn't matter so much.'

She always tries to finish work at three so that she can have time with the children. 'It's really during the school holidays that having a nanny is a godsend,' says Ann. 'Without her I just couldn't work, and you can't tell a regular client that you won't be able to help them for three or four months each year because you have to look after the kids. That doesn't look very professional, does it?

'There hasn't been one problem yet with these arrangements, touch wood,' says Ann. 'And if I need to do more work in the day, then I simply put in a couple more hours after the kids have gone to bed.'

How to stop family problems before they occur

As soon as possible, and preferably before you begin your homeworking career, it is important to bring as many potential family difficulties into the open where they can be dealt with and solutions discussed. The longer problems lie concealed the more resentment and frustration build up.

- First, establish a set of ground rules so that everyone in the family knows what they now can and cannot do. Such rules might include deciding when your office hours are going to be, which parts of the house are off-limits to children during office hours, who can answer the phone and when, how loud the television can be, when the children can play noisily outside, and what does it mean if your office door is closed? It is always good to have a pre-thought-out plan to cope with any emergencies, major and minor.

- When there are conflicts of interest, be prepared to trade off with others members of the family. Learn to make concessions. For instance, your teenage daughter will not take kindly to being told she cannot make a phone call during your office hours, but perhaps she could be allowed a couple of ten-minute calls at certain times during the week? She may not like that but it's better than nothing and it prevents you being seen as a total 'dictator'.

- Hold family meetings regularly and revise the rules if you have to. Circumstances change and so do people. Keep on altering the family routine until a comfortable balance is achieved between different people's interests.

- Where you can, include the family in your work. Bounce ideas off them or ask how they would go about doing a job. The more involved they feel the more co-operation you are likely to receive from them.

Use a family scheduling calendar

Try and involve your family in scheduling your work, incorporating all of the family's needs into a master schedule. To do this hang a large calendar or wall chart at a convenient place in the house, perhaps in the kitchen.

On this, every member of the family should be encouraged to enter details of their timetable for the week ahead and preferably for the next month. Use different coloured pens to distinguish between you.

Every week hold a family meeting at which you thrash out any clashes of interest. If someone forgets or can't be bothered to enter their details on the scheduling calendar, they shouldn't be surprised if they lose out when it comes to borrowing cars and the like. All family members must respect the time of others. This can be a particular problem for teenagers who can't see why you can't pick them up from a shopping trip, even if you have a business meeting at the same time!

Action point

Right now, arrange a time with other family members when you will sit down to talk about your homeworking career. At this meeting you will resolve any problems there might be about you working from home and decide on the ground rules that you are all going to abide by.

How to make more time for your family

Everyone has 168 hours in the week. Some of this you will spend working, some with your family and some on the mundane chores of keeping a household together. Obviously the less time that you spend doing housework the more time you have for your family and work. As 'Superwoman' Shirley Conran remarked life really is 'too short to stuff a mushroom'.

Action point
Add up the time you spend doing each of the activities below

Activity	Hours spent each week
Shopping	
Washing clothes	
Washing up	
Cooking	
Ironing	
Household cleaning	
Childcare	_____
Total	_____

Use your housework hours
Seek ways to reduce the time you spend doing household chores. This you can either do by delegating them to others, or minimising the time it takes to do a job by developing short cuts.

- Don't be possessive about particular tasks or parts of the house. Start talking about 'our' kitchen rather than 'my' kitchen. The stained top of the coffee table isn't just your responsibility, it's everyone's.

- Make up a communal file that contains information that helps others do the whole range of jobs that would normally be left to just one person.

- Develop interchangeable roles in the household. There is no reason why a male should always take the car to the garage, or a female do all of the shopping.

- Share the unpleasant tasks. You can quickly become resentful if after you have had a hard day working from home, someone else wants to know why the bath or the toilet hasn't been cleaned.

- From an early age, teach your children to tidy up after themselves and to be responsible for taking on some of the smaller jobs around the house, such as watering the plants.

- Cook complicated and time-consuming meals less often.

- Cook large amounts of a favourite dish and freeze it. Then all you need do is microwave or heat it up.

- Soak dishes rather than trying to clean them when food is stuck to the plate.

- Reduce the number of shopping trips you make.

- Organise your shopping trips more effectively so that you bring home everything you need and do not have to make extra trips for forgotten items.

- Rather than doing all your household cleaning at one go, break it into smaller sections which can be fitted into your work breaks. Cleaning the bath or wash basin could slot into one of your ten-minute breaks.

Case study – up with the lark

When John began work from home, the rest of the family suffered. The two young children were forbidden to ever utter a word during office hours, which were often extended well beyond the traditional five o'clock finish. The television in the living room had to be turned down to the minimum so as not to disturb John. He even stopped helping around the house, using his heavy workload as an excuse. In fact he quickly became unbearable. The problem was solved only after compromises were made.

Now John gets up an hour and a half earlier so that he manages a good hour's work before the children wake. He also ensures that the children have a free hour when they come home from school. Then they can do what they want, letting off steam, being noisy and generally being children. But John insists that if he gets a phone call at these times, the children stay quiet.

How to say 'no' to others

The calls made on your time by others such as neighbours and family will be one of the biggest interruptions that you will encounter. Homeworkers are often approached by others who want little favours. For instance, letting in a delivery man, holding on to keys or keeping an eye on their house. It is highly important that you control and protect your time.

Every time you succumb to someone else's interruption it costs you money, and if you constantly give into the demands of others then you will become frustrated and stressed. So never be afraid to say no to others and do not beat around the bush. Make no the first word in your sentence of rejection, but soften the blow by making a concession. This is particularly important when dealing with your children's requests. Always explain why you have said no and emphasise what the benefits are to the family, for instance you will finish a piece of work sooner and have the weekend free, or you will be able to use the additional money to take them on holiday or go out to a restaurant.

Unfortunately there are times when you do have to be firm and demand that, because of an important piece of work, the rules must be temporarily changed. When that happens, do not forget to thank your family for their co-operation, perhaps rewarding them with some treat, or doing a trade-off.

Try not to make spur of the moment decisions. Tell people you will think about the situation and check whether it will fit in with your schedule. If you do this you won't be forced into going back on a promise at a later date, just because it was easier to say yes three months before.

MOTIVATING YOURSELF TO WORK

When you work from home there is no-one else to really motivate you but yourself. And no matter how enthusiastic you are about your work, there will be times when you will flag and not want to get on with the job. Then you must be your own foreman and make sure that you stick your nose to the grindstone when you have to. The following techniques won't work for everyone, but they can be very stimulating when you are in a trough.

Fresh-from-the-bed work session

When you wake in the morning do not let anything distract you from starting work, this includes washing, breakfasting and dressing. Throw on a dressing-gown and just head for your desk. Then after forty-five minutes or so take the break you need and clean yourself up...if you want to.

This technique not only helps you avoid distractions, but is highly motivating. You achieve something right from the beginning of the day, which is 'money in the bank' should problems prevent you from working later on. After your first break you are then doubly keen to build on your flying start. If you go through the usual daily routine of a relaxing bath and breakfasting, an hour can drift past, gone forever, and you are not yet at your desk.

Unfinished business

When you stop work in the evening, break the general rule of clearing your desk for the day and leave something on the desk undone. Finish work in the middle of a sentence or halfway through a design. Then in the morning you have no hesitation about what to do first. There it is in front of you. You get off to a rolling start instead of moving from a standstill.

Buffer zone tactics

Make some distinction between work and home by creating a buffer zone between the two. Then when it is time for work you can leave home behind and 'go out' to work just like everyone else. Conversely at night you do the opposite. Many homeworkers find that this is particularly important when they begin working from home. To do this, recreate a set of rituals to replace those that you have left behind in the traditional workplace. You could use the following rituals as your props:

- Transfer possessions from your old office into your new home office. A familiar clock, pot plant, calendar or ornament all play their part in tricking your mind into thinking you are back in those old surroundings.

- One of the great delights of working from home is not having to dress up, but this makes some homeworkers too relaxed. Overcome this by dressing in work clothes such as suit, or jacket, which makes you feel as though you are going out to work. At first it may seem strange dressing up to walk only a few yards from one part of the house to another, but the idea works. When you are more confident in your new environment you can slouch around in jeans and T-shirt.

Action point
How will you create a buffer zone, between home and work? Write your ideas down in the space below.

Case history – Simon's morning ritual
Some homeworkers take their morning rituals to extremes. For instance, every day when Simon, a translator, wakes at seven, he washes, shaves, puts on a suit and goes down to breakfast. When he has finished, at 8.15, he picks up his briefcase, leaves through the front door of the house, walks down by the side of the house and in through the back door. Walking into the kitchen is akin to arriving at reception, now he can head for his upstairs office, ready to start work for the day. It may sound bizarre, but for Simon his ritual works.

Procrastination
Procrastination is putting off doing what we have to do. It has been called the 'thief of time' and for those who let this particular villain into their lives, minutes, days and hours will quickly vanish. Sadly, everyone succumbs to it from time to time. When the put-off tasks are trivial, then no real harm is done, but when they are large and important, real problems can develop.

Why procrastination occurs

You are most likely to put off doing something when you have a fear of doing it, either because of the consequences or because the task could be psychologically painful. If there is no-one else to take on these 'put off' jobs, then they either go undone, or are left until the last minute. What is more, they tend to irritatingly hang around, reminding us that they ought to be done, making us feel guilty and taking our concentration from other tasks.

For all homeworkers and anyone who works by themselves, it is extremely important to overcome this problem. Do not for an instant see it as a harmless idiosyncrasy. Once it has become a habit procrastination will seriously affect your work. You should do everything to stamp it out. Thankfully there are a number of tried and tested techniques for doing just that.

How to beat procrastination

Ask yourself what is the worst thing that can happen if you do the job you are putting off. Usually the worst result would be a few moments of embarrassment and no more.

- Can you make yourself feel more confident by making better preparations, such as acquiring additional facts that will let you present your case better?

- Imagine yourself actually doing the task you are putting off— successfully, confidently and expertly. See yourself making that call, writing that speech or pitching for business.

- Do not avoid the most difficult problems. They almost certainly won't go away and are likely to get far worse. So, set aside a specially designated time, perhaps each day, perhaps just once or twice a week when you will do that job you have been putting off.

- Decide on one area of your homeworking life where you tend to put off doing things. Make it one of your top jobs to defeat procrastination in this area.

- Do not try and tackle too many tasks and activities at once. Many problems can be resolved by concentrated effort.

- Do not try to be a perfectionist. Doing the very best you can is commendable, but perfection cannot be achieved. At some point you must say enough is enough and finish the task.

- If you put off a project because it appears very large, try the 'Salami Technique' — slice up the project into smaller segments. These slices could be as 'thin' as checking a phone number and address, deciding on a time when you will make that telephone call, and then making it. If the project is a very large one, then the list you make of 'slices' will be very long. As you complete each segment, the project moves slowly but irrevocably forward.

- In a similar vein, promise to tackle the unpleasant task you are putting off for just ten minutes each day. You usually end up doing more than this, but if you only do the ten minutes then at least you have taken a small step.

- If a project seems overwhelming then just start anywhere. The beginning isn't always the best place, the middle may be an easier or more convenient place. Work your way out to the other sections when your brain has warmed up.

- Make two lists. On one are the reasons why you could be procrastinating, while on the other are the benefits of not putting off the job. This column should far outweigh the other list of lame excuses.

- If you have a particular problem starting a job, keep temptation at bay by making sure there is nothing around to stop you tackling it. Biscuits, coffee and magazines should all be banished from the office. They should be kept as treats and only taken when deserved and in one of your designated work breaks. Use your daily schedule to keep you on the straight and narrow.

- When you go to bed make sure that there are no distractions to take your mind off work the next morning. For instance, if you are the tidy sort who likes the house shipshape do chores like the washing up the night before. If you do not, then you will start feeling guilty about not doing the washing up, or cleaning and will either begin the next day with a cleaning binge which takes you away from work, or feel guilty about not doing it, which means you can't concentrate fully on your work.

- Above all do things now. They rarely get better or go away on their own. Action is movitating and positive, just sitting back lets others, and other things, take control of your life.

Don't expect to eradicate procrastination from your homeworking life completely, or all at once. Particularly when starting out to change this habit, you must be tough with yourself, after all you are forcing yourself to do something you don't want to do. On the other hand don't be a masochist, so don't go through this forcing procedure more than once a day.

Action point

In the space below write down three work-related tasks and three personal tasks that you are putting off.

1._____

2._____

3._____

Pick one of these jobs and tackle it now. Use some of the anti-procrastination techniques described above if they will help.

How not to be a workaholic

Anyone who is self-employed will sometimes need to work long hours to finish a project. This is simply part of being professional. But when work becomes the mainstay of life it is a problem.

And when you work from home it is all to easy to stay at your desk until late into the night, or just keep popping into the office to finish something off. And if you hear the chattering of an incoming fax, can you put off looking at it until the morning?

Workaholism is not a virtue and should not be seen as such. It doesn't mean that you are highly productive. If work so dominates your life, it may be that bad work methods mean that you cannot get on top of the job, or you have a subsconscious desire to be overworked, or because you feel you have nothing better to do.

Everyone should balance work and leisure. If you don't then your work will not only suffer in the long term but you will be in danger of becoming a first class bore.

- Make sure that you have plenty of interests outside your home. Put aside at least one evening every week or fortnight when you will go out. Arrange to regularly meet friends down at the pub or restaurant, and take a trip to the theatre or cinema. If you go out you can still end up talking about work, but at least you can't be doing it.

- It may not always be best to involve your family in trying to break you from your habit of overwork. If you say that you will go out with them and then disappoint them again and again because you can't go, you will be doing no-one any favours.

- Try to find some means of creating a barrier between your office and the rest of the house. The same sort of buffer zone that motivates others to work can also be used as a barrier to help the potential workaholic switch off.

Case history – Phil's reminder

Every Friday night Phil pins a small sign on his office door, just at eye level where he can't miss it. The sign reads 'Office closed until 9 am Monday. Now go away and do something else.' It is just Phil's way of reminding himself with a smile that there are things in life other than a drawing board and pens. It reminds him to keep his weekends clear.

Case history – Jeremy locks the door

When Jeremy began working from home he found that instead of clocking off at five o'clock, he was carrying on late into the evening, finishing at nine or ten, but even later if he had a large project on the boil.

His work hours led to constant arguments with his wife, Janet, complaining bitterly that though he was home all day she saw him far less than when he used to commute into town. But no matter how precarious his relationship became, Jeremy always found just one more thing to do before he finished for the night. Only when his wife threatened to leave him, did Jeremy decide that drastic methods were required.

He fitted his office door with a lock. Now when he finishes work he locks his door and hands the key over to his wife. The result is he can't get in, even if he wanted to. The system works perfectly for him and his family.

Case history – Malcolm creates a motivational montage

To keep himself firmly focused on his work, Malcolm creates a motivational montage. He collects pictures from brochures and magazines of things that he wants to own or do. These images are as colourful, bright and energetic as he can find and are of things that *really* motivate him – in Malcom's case a new car, computer and a holiday in Bali. All these he sticks on a pinboard which he puts on the wall in front of him.

On each picture he writes the date by which he wants to own or have done something. Now, when Malcolm looks up from his desk he sees the pictures which give him just that little extra incentive to work another quarter or half hour, just when he was ready to pack in for the day.

If an image ceases to inspire him, or better still he achieves it, then he changes it for another that motivates him more. Malcolm even carries this technique over into his travel time, by having a picture of something he really wants stuck on the dashboard of his car.

A variation of this montage is to also include bad things you *don't* want to happen to you (pictures of homelessness, illness, poverty). Very often fear of something is a stronger motivational cost than a desire for it.

9
Keeping Healthy and Safe

SPOKEN FROM EXPERIENCE

'Early to rise and early to bed makes a male healthy and wealthy and dead.' James Thurber.

'One of the minor pleasures of life is to be slightly ill.' Harold Nicholson.

'Moderation is a fatal thing. Nothing succeeds like excess.' Oscar Wilde.

'The amount of sleep required by the average person is about five minutes more.' Max Kauffman.

YOUR MAJOR ASSET: YOU

When you work from home and for yourself, you are your own best asset. There is no-one else to take over when you fall sick or feel off colour. It should therefore go without saying that you ought to do everything you can to make sure you stay in the pink, and that includes creating a safe and healthy environment in which to work.

But, when you work from home you can often be more at risk than your office-based counterparts because you do not have pressure from trade unions and health and safety legislation that employers have, to develop an office that is safe and healthy to work in.

The health problems that you are most likely to encounter will come from: your computer which can affect your eyes, skin, wrists and arms; a bad working position which gives you backache and shoulder pains; and stress, which often arises from bad working methods.

THE COMPUTER AND YOUR HEALTH

Since their use became widespread, computers have been variously blamed, rightly and wrongly, for various complaints and health problems.

- There have been worries about the magnetic and electrical emissions from computers, though The National Radiological Protection Board says that there is no risk from VDU screens because their emission levels are so low. Some authorities claim that VDU emissions are responsible for miscarriages in pregnant women, though research results are contradictory. If you are worried, you may feel it wise to limit the hours you spend at the computer screen to just one or two. Some companies do produce radiation screens which are claimed to offer protection.

- There is evidence that prolonged VDU use can worsen existing vision problems and long periods spent in front of a screen are said to affect your night vision as your eyes take increasingly longer to send visual information collected by the eye to the brain.

- Nearly one-third of office workers using VDUs suffer from eye-strain, tiredness and pains in the back, shoulder and neck, according to a recent opinion poll.

- About 8% of VDU users suffer from rashes and other skin conditions such as acne and rosacea. These symptoms will generally appear two to four hours after starting work at the VDU, but then generally disappear overnight.

THE PROBLEM OF RSI

With the widespread and frequent usage of computers, Repetitive Strain Injury or RSI has very much become an occupational hazard. The rapid and repeated movements of the arm and wrist, associated with using a computer keyboard or typewriter can soon tire and inflame the tendons and muscles of the arms, wrists and hands. If the condition is mild the discomfort and pain soon disappear, but if it is severe then you can literally be crippled for months, unable to lift or hold anything and certainly not able to type. At this stage permanent injury can be done.

If you ever suffer from shooting pains or numbness of the hands while typing then you should cut down on the time that you spend typing. If you ever have pain when you are not typing then you should seek medical help.

What causes RSI?

Badly designed computer equipment and office furniture which is incorrectly positioned are two of the main reasons why office workers can become injured. Some of the main points for positioning your chair and desk have been covered in Chapter 4.

How to avoid RSI

Everyone who uses a keyboard a great deal of their working week is at risk from RSI, but a few simple precautions should reduce your chances of falling prey to this uncomfortable ailment.

- Use well designed computer and office equipment and make sure that your chair and desk are well positioned. See Chapter 4.

- Position the keyboard on the desk so that your arms are roughly parallel to the floor when typing. Your elbows should be angled at between 70 and 90 degrees.

- When you sit comfortably at your desk, the computer screen should be between 35 and 60 cm away. Ideally you should be able to move the screen to the left and right and tilt it up and down so that there is no glare on the screen and so that you don't need to contort yourself to see it.

- The centre of the screen should be placed so that you look down at it from an angle of about 15 to 20 degrees.

- Trade unions recommend that you only use a keyboard for a maximum of four to five hours every day. It is well to follow their advice.

- Research suggests that taking short breaks frequently is better for you than taking fewer longer ones. When you work a lot at the computer face, take a rest break of 12-15 minutes every hour. This can easily be fitted into your daily schedule. Take some of this break time to exercise and stretch your arms, hands and fingers.

Eight ways to help your eyes
Eighty per cent of VDU users are said to suffer from eyesight problems. So it is worth making sure that your eyes stay up to scratch.

- Take regular eye check-ups. Uncorrected vision defects can be made worse by VDU use.

- Adjust your computer screen so that it is not too bright or the contrast too harsh as this tends to tire the eyes. Experiment until you find a restful combination.

- Make sure that the characters on screen are large enough for you to read easily and without peering. Some computer software allows you to alter the size of characters to a level that suits you.

- If glare is a problem on your screen then an anti-glare screen can be bought, though this will make the screen darker and slightly more difficult to read. Some of these also cut down on static.

- Clean your computer screen regularly so that there is no build up of grime to obscure and blur the characters on screen.

- Make sure you take those rest breaks every hour. Even if your hands, wrists and arms don't feel tired, you should give your eyes a rest.

- There are two basic ways in which characters are displayed on your screen—light characters on a dark background or dark characters on a light background. Some researchers believe that the former is more soothing on the eyes while others think that the latter is better because it resembles a printed page. Research is so far limited and so for the moment how you set your screen is a matter of personal preference.

- Don't drink too much alcohol if you are doing a lot of computer work. It slows down your visual reactions and can contribute to eye-strain.

OTHER TIPS FOR A HEALTHY OFFICE

Increase the level of ventilation. Open a window if you can, this not only has the benefit of letting in fresh air, but also releases any general staleness and chemical fumes from the photocopier, fax or new furniture and carpets.

- Though the chemical fumes released from your photocopier and fax won't be so bad as in a larger office, make sure that both machines are well maintained to minimise their emissions.

- The humidity of your office should be about 40-50%. Put a saucer of water near to a radiator to increase it to this level. If the air in your office is too dry then you could suffer from problems to your skin and contact lens.

THE IMPORTANCE OF SLEEP

When you work from home it is easy to burn the candle at both ends by working late into the night and starting early in the morning. If you are to be at your most effective you do need to have a good night's sleep.

If insomnia is a problem, don't resort to sleeping tablets. They help only in the short term and can lead to greater problems. If going to sleep is particularly difficult then finish work as early as you can to let your brain and body 'slow down' before you go to bed.

Only go to bed when you feel tired and make sure that your bed is warm and comfortable. Try some good old fashioned healthy exercise, this not only makes you fitter but tires you out as well.

With all this said, the irritability and tiredness that go with lack of sleep can also be the result of too much sleep. Most people need between six and a half and eight hours sleep each night though many of us could cut down on our sleep by 90-120 minutes each night. If you want to reduce your sleeping hours do this gradually getting up fifteen or twenty minutes earlier for a week, then doing the same the next week and so on for about six weeks. Should you begin to feel that your work performance is suffering then don't reduce your sleeping time any more until you are comfortable at this present level. Reducing your sleep in this way can actually improve its quality, though you may find it harder to wake up in the morning.

Naps

Take a tip from Churchill, if you feel tired, take a nap—but don't feel guilty. A fifteen or twenty minute doze after lunch can re-energise you so that you are brighter and sharper for the work ahead. However, don't use this as an excuse to slack off, naps will help you, but don't abuse them.

PROBLEMS OF STRESS

Most people think that tension is bad for you and your business, but tension is really the force that gets jobs done. If everything was quiet then there would be no pressure to achieve. What you need is positive tension not the negative sort that produces harmful stress, heart conditions, panic attacks and generally slows us down.

Unfortunately just because you work from home doesn't mean you won't ever suffer from stress. You may remove some of the main causes of stress in your working environment, such as irritating bosses and colleagues, corporate politics and traffic jams, but there are still factors which will create stress.

Are you suffering from stress?

Stress can be combated, but it is important to recognise the signs when they first start to occur.

- Have you recently become more impatient, ever ready to leap down the throat of any family member if they make a suggestion you don't agree with, cause a disturbance or inconvenience you?

- Do you feel swamped by the amount of work you have to do?

- Are you sleeping normally, or do you now lie awake with your head full of the day's problems?

- Do you put off doing jobs that you know you have to do, and so feel yourself becoming 'uptight'?

- Do you welcome interruptions that stop you from working, but then feel guilty about the work you haven't done?

- Are you trying to be a perfectionist all of the time?

- Do you end up jumping from job to job, because you know you have so little time to do all of them?

Why are you so stressed?

For long-term control it is important to identify those areas which are causing your stress. When you know what they are you can start to do something about them. These are some of the most likely causes:

- A bad working environment. If you don't feel comfortable in your office, you won't want to go in there to work (see Chapters 3 and 4).

- Poor organisation and time management. If you organise your work life badly you won't be so productive, you'll miss deadlines and produce lower quality work. All of these add to your stress levels (see Chapters 6 and 7).

- Loneliness. We all need social contact at some time (see Chapter 8).

- Pressure from your family and friends. Perhaps they don't take you seriously or want you to give them more time (see Chapter 8).

- Too much work. Better to have too much than too little, but you can soon become avalanched by jobs. When you work on your own there is no-one else around to lighten the load, but try and separate work from home. Create that all important buffer zone (see Chapter 8).

- Too little work. This is a problem that is closely linked with financial worries. The only answer is to go on a promotional campaign (see Chapter 10).

How to manage stress

You can reduce the level of stress you feel by organising your office and your time, but some residual stress always remains. It is important to manage this so that it doesn't develop out of hand and begin to affect your productivity.

- Regular exercise not only makes you fitter, brighter, healthier, but also calmer. If you don't want to enter into organised sports, then take a few walks of at least twenty minutes (an hour would be better). These can be fitted in during lunch breaks or even first thing in the morning to launch the day off to a flying start and a brisk walk is highly unlikely to cause you any injuries. Cycling, swimming and running are all good exercise and stress releasers.

- Take up a hobby that will absorb you. It should be something you have sufficient time for and different enough from your daily work to relax your mind.

- Use music to relax. Many claims are made for the harmonies of Baroque music which are said to be particularly good at relaxing you, lowering muscle tension and blood pressure. The music should be at about 60 beats to the minute.

   You can also use music to help you when you have a diffficult task to do. For instance, if you have to make a problem phone call, motivate yourself by listening to some stirring music, perhaps classical, which makes you feel on top of the world.

- Relaxation and meditation exercise are a great help. Classes are held at most local colleges. If you don't want to make that sort of commitment then there are a few simple exercises that you can do at home to help yourself relax and stay calm, when others are losing their heads. Don't feel that you are a crank doing them. Many highly successful business people, politicians and sportsmen and women do exactly the same thing. Fifteen to twenty minutes of relaxation exercises each day is time well spent.

SEVEN STEPS TO RELAXATION

- Take a few deep breaths inhaling through your nose and then exhaling slowly through the mouth.

- Waggle your jaw around.

- Lie on the floor and stretch out as far as you can with arms and legs. Then relax.

- Screw your face up tight for a few seconds then release the tension and feel the relaxation.

- Do the same with your fists.

- Roll your head upon your neck in circles from left to right, then right to left.

- Roll your shoulders backwards and forwards.

A quick relaxer for back and neck

Lie flat on the floor in a quiet place where you won't be disturbed. Tilt your pelvis so that all of your back is lying flat on the floor (check with your hand that the small of your back is touching the floor). Lengthen your spine by moving your head forward so that your chin is tucked up. Lie like this for a few minutes with your arms by your sides, palms face up and with your eyes closed.

Case history – Ross takes on too much

Ross had always been a doer. And because he found that he was far more productive working from home, it gave him extra time to take on a few extra jobs in the community, standing on a committee here and another one there.

He handled all of the responsibilities well, but then a big contract came along which Ross pitched for and landed. Completing the contract would take up a lot of Ross's time, but he thought that he could just about juggle all of his other community jobs and work. Very soon he found he couldn't.

He started missing committee meetings, and skimping on a section of the contract work here and there. Ross was beginning to feel the strain, but he still thought he could do his committee work, after all he had been elected to do it and there was no-one else to take it on.

To make sure that he finished the contract on time, Ross worked every hour that he could and tolerated no disturbances which could spoil his concentration.

If the children were noisy he shouted at them, and then would have a row with Marion, his wife, about what he had done. Eventually Ross finished the big project and surprisingly on time, even though he had to work all through the night to do it.

Even though he was a well organised homeworker, Ross's productivity and quality of work slipped as he took on too much. His sense of community responsibility had stopped him from reducing his committee work, at least while he had extra work to do, putting both himself and his family under intolerable pressure.

FOOD AND DRINK

With the kitchen only a quick walk away, there is a great temptation to drink vast amounts of tea and coffee. If you take a break every fifty minutes or so and have a drink, you could be taking in ten to fifteen cups of coffee or tea a day. If you are such a drinkaholic, start substituting every third cup for a drink of squash or water. You'll probably feel less irritable.

Likewise if you are a dedicated snacker, working from home can soon see you pack on the pounds with the biscuit tin so near at hand. Learn to break the habit gently by cutting down on the number of snacks you take and eating low calorie healthy snacks such as apples rather than chocolate bars.

When you eat, try to do so away from the place where you work. This not only gives you a chance to take a well earned break, but means you are less likely to spill food or drink over your computer, papers or designs.

Homeworker fast food

Quickly prepared snacks such as the ones listed below save the homeworker time and are healthy. These are some of the snacks that can be made first thing in the morning (don't leave it until later otherwise you just won't bother to make up the salads, or clean the potatoes) and be 'picked at' throughout the day. They will give you all the energy you need to make it through even the hardest working day.

Baked potatoes	Dried fruit
Raw vegetables	Baked beans
Fruit	Green salads
Yoghurt	Bean salads
Low fat cheese	Crispbreads

KEEP YOUR OFFICE GREEN

A few plants in your office are not only restful but can reduce static and can clean the air of pollutants that might be emitted by office equipment. It doesn't really matter what plants you choose, but as a rule of thumb the more foliage they have the better they are at cleaning the air.

AVOIDING ACCIDENTS

Cables are inevitable with any electrical equipment and as soon as you accumulate fax, answer machine, computer and extension leads, then there are many, all waiting to trip up the unwary. But don't tuck cables under carpets. Not only do you damage the carpet, but won't be aware of the potential fire or electrical hazard if the cable becomes damaged or frayed. Wherever possible run cables around the edge of the room rather than laying them over the floor, expecially in an area that you use a great deal.

If several cables do have to cross the floor, it is sensible to use an extension lead with a series of sockets at one end. Then you need to look out for the extension cable and not three or four others. If you use a long enough extension lead then you may simply be able to run it along the walls.

Heavy rubber conduits can be bought to cover cabling. These provide protection for the cable and keep it out of the way. They may look out of place in your office, but they keep cables safe, which is especially important if you have people working for you or clients visiting. Industrial tape serves the same purpose.

It should go without saying that if you ever have to work on an electrical appliance turn off the power first.

CHECKLIST

Periodically, say every three months, give your body a MOT. Look out for the following points.

- Do you suffer from eye-strain?

  Yes ☐   No ☐

- Do your eyes ever become sore, irritated or burn?

  Yes ☐   No ☐

- Do you ever suffer from blurred or double vision?

  Yes ☐   No ☐

- Since working in front of a VDU have you started perceiving colours in a different way?

  Yes ☐   No ☐

- Do you ever suffer from headaches, migraine, or nausea during or after you use your computer?

  Yes ☐   No ☐

- Do you easily become tired and irritable after a while in your office?

  Yes ☐   No ☐

- Do you have problems with your contact lens or your skin?

  Yes ☐   No ☐

- Do you suffer from back or shoulder problems?

  Yes ☐   No ☐

- Do you suffer from pains in your wrists and hands after working at the keyboard?

  Yes ☐   No ☐

10
Promoting Your Business from Home

SPOKEN FROM EXPERIENCE

'If you take out a girl and at the end of the evening, tell her that you are a terrific lover, that is *advertising*. On the other hand if you tell her that she really does need a lover and that you are the man, then that is *marketing*. But if before you can say a word, she tells you *she's* heard that you are a wonderful lover, then that's *public relations.*'

'An opportunity is as real an ingredient in business as raw material, labour or finance—but it only exists when you can see it.' Edward de Bono.

'Any fool can write a sales letter—and too many do.' Brian Holland, ad agency owner.

'There are no new ideas in advertising.' Ed McCabe, US adman.

'Nothing is more humiliating than to see idiots succeed in enterprises we have failed in.' Flaubert.

LOOKING PROFESSIONAL

For most people business is a serious matter. Consequently they do not like doing business with people who do not look business-like. It causes them to mistrust you, generally because they think you cannot do the job. This applies whether you work from a huge Central London office block or a cottage in Cheshire.

- If you look as though you are running a successful business others are more likely to give you a contract in the first place.

- All other things being equal, a contract will generally go to a business that looks the most professional and business-like. In a highly competitive world anything that gives you the edge has to be taken advantage of.

- If you look professional then you are more likely to be paid promptly when you have finished the job.

137

- If the public face of your business looks good, then in turn you will feel more confident. This is vitally important when you are just starting to work from home and may feel a little unsure.

YOUR BUSINESS NAME

You may be quite happy trading simply under your own name. It is simple, convenient, obviously doesn't require you to spend any time thinking up a business name and continually reminds customers of the name of the person in charge. If you choose to do this then don't use your initials. Peter Jones is more inviting than P. J. Jones, Plumber.

However, there are good reasons why even someone who works alone from home should trade under a business name.

- It makes your business appear larger than it is, as nobody knows exactly how many people are involved in your organisation. There is nothing wrong in doing this as long as you don't lie should clients ask. When you trade under your own name it suggests that you are either a one-man band or at least a very small company.

- A trading name adds a professional gloss to your business. Ideas that Sell sounds more impressive than Ian Phillipson Publicity Services!

- If your name is difficult to pronounce, spell or would give off the wrong impression about your business, then you should choose a business name to trade under.

What should you call your business?

Imagine potential customers running their fingers down a Yellow Pages listing. Often the only information they will use to decide to call is a name. A carefully chosen business name creates the right impression about your business.

Indeed, so important are names that highly creative think-tanks spend months developing the best name for a chocolate bar! You owe it to yourself to spend at least a few hours and preferably days doing the same for your homeworking business.

Long names may initially catch the imagination, but paradoxically they can also be more easily forgotten. Try to think of a name that sounds good to the ear and has a natural rhythm expecially if you can create a striking or unusual image. Never be tempted to use an acronym—a 'word' formed from the initial letters of another word. ICI (Imperial Chemical Industries) get away with it because they have been around for so long but SJWPS (Sandra Jones Word Processing Services) won't. Unless you are a limited company, since 1982 there has been no need to register the name that you choose for your business. It is in your own interests, however, to make certain that there are no similar businesses trading under your chosen name. If you do choose a name that is already in existence, then you could be asked to change the name by the company already using it. If you refuse then you could be sued and legally forced to stop.

Names for limited companies can be refused by Companies House. They can offer guidance on whether the name you have chosen is allowable. For instance, you cannot use certain names such as 'Royal', 'Bank', 'British' or 'International' without permission from the Department of Industry.

Action point

- Decide if you want to appear traditional, very modern, dynamic, creative, or reliable and choose a name accordingly.

- Decide if you want your business name to describe what you do, or rather to create a certain image. For instance, Upper Puddleton Photographic Services is descriptive, while 'Picture This' creates an image of a friendlier company.

- Write down all the other qualities you want your business to have or to portray. These might include: modern, original, dynamic, flexible, professional, approachable, interesting. Try and list them in order of importance.

1._____

2._____

3._____

4._____

5._____

The above is your checklist against which you will measure any name you think up. The more of these qualities that your business name suggests the better it will be at representing your business.

THE RIGHT BUSINESS ADDRESS?

Many homeworkers lose confidence when they have to declare that they work from an address that is obviously residential, like 'Dumroamin'.

When your house has both a name and a street number, there should be no identification problem. The name can just be dropped. If its name is the only thing that identifies the house, then it is easy enough to change the name to something more appropriate and in keeping with your business.

Simply write to your local Royal Mail Customer Care Office informing them that from a certain date your house will be known by its new name. The Customer Care Office will tell the local sorting office. If you inform them early enough then there should be no confusion.

You can call your house whatever you want, even Buckingham Palace, though it is sensible to make sure the name is not too similar to another house nearby. The Royal Mail should be able to tell you if there are likely to be problems.

Try to choose a name that creates the impression of size, solidity or the type of work you do, such as 'Merchant House'. Perhaps you could draw inspiration from a nearby feature such as a river, or spend twenty minutes flipping through the Yellow Pages for a likely name.

Do not be tempted to gild the lily by claiming that this is your head or regional office. If a client discovers the reality you will be laughed at.

Think twice about using a PO Box to disguise your address. It can make you look as though you have something to hide, or are going to suddenly disappear (customers are less likely to hand money over to you if they think you are going to do a moonlight flit). And don't think that using a PO Box makes you anonymous and will stop people stomping to your door. Anyone can phone the appropriate post office and find out who has been allocated that box number, though sometimes perseverence is required as not all postal workers know this information can be given out.

DESIGNING YOUR STATIONERY

Smartly dressed and professional looking sales reps do better business than scruffy ones. The same can be said about the letters you send out. They are your sales staff.

First impressions do count. When your letter lands on the desk of a potential supplier, customer or bank manager it might be their first contact with you. Your letterhead can either make them confident in your services... or nervous. Every business should have a carefully designed letterhead.

Many high street printers create letterheads at reasonable cost. All you do is supply the relevant information which is slotted into a standard format. This kind of letterhead conveys information but it doesn't 'sell' your services.

How to design your letterheads

You should realise that your letter will be just one of many that your customers and suppliers receive every day. You need to make your letter stand out from the pack and be noticed and at the same time contain relevant information about you and your business.

Your letterhead should show your name or trading name, a logo if you have one, your address, telephone and fax numbers (including STD codes) and membership of relevant associations. If you trade under a business name then by law your own name must be included.

- If your annual turnover is above the VAT threshold, currently £46,000, then you must register for VAT and display your VAT registration number on your stationery. If your turnover is below the threshold there is still an advantage in registering.

  This will give you a VAT number that you can quote on your letterhead, which suggests to clients and suppliers that your business is bringing in at least £46,000. On the downside you have more paperwork to do.

- Do not think that the more garish your letterhead the better it works. It will certainly catch the recipient's eye, but also churn their stomach. They won't think you are professional, indeed they will think the reverse.

- Use only good quality white, cream or light grey paper, about 100gm in weight. Other shades and colours may look attractive to you but others can find them irritating. Darker colours also make words more difficult to read. 'Safe' colours are best.

- Buy envelopes and continuation sheets in a matching colour. Consider having your business name printed on the envelopes for a very professional look. There are restrictions on what can be printed on envelopes. Check with the Post Office about what is allowable.

- Add a line to your letterhead, which spells out what you do. This could be as varied as 'Television Researcher', 'Professional publicity', or 'High quality graphic design'.

- If you want a logo, try not to be clichéd. If you are a writer, don't use the image of a pen, likewise avoid a brush if you are an artist—be more imaginative, this is particularly important if you are in a creative occupation.

- Don't use embossed paper. It is more difficult to type and print on. If you do use embossed paper then make sure the lettering is picked out with colour, otherwise no one will be able to read the information.

- If you are extrovert, consider putting your photograph on the letterhead. This is different and people will certainly remember your letter. Make sure the photograph is professionally taken.

- When you have decided what elements you want on your letterhead, ask a professional graphic artist to design it for you. The cost-conscious alternative is to ask students at an art college to take the job. Contact a tutor.

- After your letterheads have been delivered, keep control of them. Correspondence sent out by others on your letterheads could be potentially embarrassing, or even legally enforceable.

Action point
Begin to collect other people's letterheads. Analyse what is good and bad about each of them. What can you learn or even copy from them?

Sketch out ten different logos or visual ideas for your letterheads. It doesn't matter if you can't draw. Choose the ideas you think best and ask yourself if they fit in with the image you want to create for your business.

Designing your business card
These are an essential item. Business cards are no good sitting on your shelves, they need to be out in the wide, wide world working for you. You should never be shy in giving them out to people who might be able to use your services.

- Business cards should be designed in conjunction with your letterheads so that you portray a co-ordinated image.

- Use a credit card size. People are used to credit cards, so your business card looks right. They are also more noticeable than smaller ones and give extra design space.

Compliment slips
These aren't necessary when you are first starting working from home. If you need the occasional compliment slip you may be able to contrive one from your letterheads by cutting off the bottom section of the page.

PROMOTING YOURSELF

If you don't let people know you are around how are they going to do business with you? This is especially important in the first year of your homeworking life, but even when you are well into your stride you must continue to search for new customers, or at least have some in the pipeline. Never be complacent that you have too much business. Better

Ideas That sell

Words That Work

Ian Phillipson

1 Homend Hopkilns
Cradley
Malvern
Worcs. WR13 5NW
Tel: 0886 880532

Professional publicity you can afford

ARCHITECTS
SURVEYORS
and DESIGN
CONSULTANTS

Steve Meredith

PARTNER

Courtyard Studio

Lyttleton House

Abbey Road

Great Malvern

Worcestershire

WR14 3ES

Tel: 0684 568929

HARCOURT DESIGN

Fig. 7. Two examples of business cards that sell an image of their companies. Both are credit card size, though one is upright and the other landscape.

that way than too little. If you have too much then you should look at either employing staff or subcontracting work.

Though advertising in the local, national or trade press may seem the obvious means of contacting potential customers, think carefully before paying out cash for ad space. General press advertising has its place, but is an expensive and often ineffective way of reaching customers—most homeworkers will not have the promotional budgets for large and widespread advertising campaigns in any case. However, there are ways of promoting your home business cost-effectively.

Don't wait for the world to come to you

Many homeworkers have seen their businesses killed off at any early date simply because they have waited for the world to come to them. Without the traditional contacts of the workplace and with no signs, or nameplates to advertise themselves, homeworkers simply have to go out into the world and sell.

And the more you get out into the business world, showing your face and making contacts the more likely you are to get business, and it is always better to have too much work than have too little. So be sure to build regular work hunting sessions into your daily or weekly timetable.

But be sensible in your chase for work. Concentrate your efforts on projects and jobs that are most likely to come good (though take a chance sometimes on an off-the-wall exciting project, but don't rely on it) otherwise you will have to do twice or three times the work for the same reward.

How to advertise in a directory

Taking on a business phone line gives you a single-line listing in the Yellow Pages. Should you decide to advertise in its pages (and 96% of 'business information users' are said to look through them) there are certain guidelines which should help generate more response.

- Avoid a single-line entry that just gives your name, your address and number. It is next to useless when it comes to pulling in business. Instead take the largest display ad that you can afford. Ads of this size are really the only ones that are read because they are the most obvious and no-one wants to plough through twenty or thirty single-line entries (think about how you use the Yellow Pages). This costs more but is far more effective as a sales medium because directory users go first to the more prominent display ads and ignore the small and very numerous lineage ads. In business it pays to be noticed.

- Never run an ad in a newspaper or elsewhere that says you can find us in the Yellow Pages. Why direct potential clients to the place where your competitiors are advertising?

- Do your best to make your ad work its hardest. You should lay it out using bold graphics and in a strong black box. Make your telephone number as big as possible and if the relevant directory allows colour then use it. It stands out from the crowd. It is worth using a good designer to create the right effect, though a printshop with desktop publishing equipment can easily do this kind of work.

- When you write ad copy don't use clichés like 'We care more'. Make yourself different. Think of all the benefits your customer gains from using you and include them in your ad.

- Use powerful, persuasive words. According to research by Yale University the twelve most persuasive words are:

You	Health
Money	Safety
Save	Have
New	Discovery
Results	Proven
Easy	Guarantee

To this you can add others such as Free, Exclusive, Win, Special Offer, 50% Off.

- If you can, use a photograph or drawing to illustrate someone using your service or product.

- Tell the customer what they must do next. For instance, ring your 24-hour message line.

- Consider running several ads in different sections of the directory if this is appropriate.

- Don't use humour. When opening a directory they are just looking for a telephone number and want it quickly, so they aren't really in the mood for jokes. Remember that anyone consulting a directory wants to be able to receive a fast telephone response that is immediate and reassures them that you are the right person to do business with.

- When clients phone, ask where they found your name. Alternatively, your directory ad can ask callers to ask for a specific but fictitious name, which pinpoints where they got your name. The caller won't know that the person doesn't exist and you just say that the person isn't available.

- If it seems appropriate offer a credit card facility. When you accept credit cards you make it easier and quicker for a customer or client to pay because they can complete the transaction by phone or fax, using their unique card number.

WRITING LETTERS THAT SELL

The most cost-effective way of persuading potential clients to use you is with a well written and targeted sales letter. Of the letters you send out, those seeking business will often be the most important. These main points should help you write a better sales letter:

- It should go without saying that all your letters and business correspondence should be typed. Other than hastily scribbled memos, there is no place for handwriting in business communications.

- Pinpoint those people who need your services. Identify them by name and use it in your letter. If you don't know the person to write to, phone up the company switchboard and ask for the name of the 'Marketing Director', 'Personnel Officer' or whoever is most appropriate.

- Whenever possible, write the letter from a 'you' not an 'I' point of view.

- Tell the reader what benefits they will receive if they use your services. You should by now have a good idea what benefits a client will receive when they use your business.

- Make every word in your letter count. Generally a long letter that keeps the reader reading till the last full stop will outperform a short but less well written letter that loses their interest. Writing a boring letter is a sin, but don't be outrageous for the sake of it. Be outrageous only if it will bring in more business.

- If you can give supporting evidence of the work that you have done in the past, do so. It gives the potential client confidence in using your services. No-one likes to be the only one in the water.

Avoiding mistakes in your letters and literature

If no-one else is around to check your work then you must take double the care to ensure you do not send out letters and materials which contain spelling and typing errors or any other mistakes.

- Minimise the number of mistakes you make in the first place. The fewer you make the fewer you have to correct.

- If you have a mental block about the spelling of a particular word, type the word correctly and stick it next to your computer. You will soon learn how to spell it. Repeat the process with other words that give you trouble. If you use a computer and wordprocessor don't rely on its spellchecker as it cannot tell the difference between words such as 'there' or 'their' which are spelt correctly, but simply used in the wrong place.

- When you have written a letter or other document, read it out aloud. Pay particular attention to long words and those with peculiar spellings. You will soon pick up on any nonsense you have written.

- Many people find it easier to read from a printed hard copy, rather than off the computer screen. Correcting from a sheet of paper is well worth the extra time if you avoid mistakes.

- When working on a project of many pages, print out your work on long lengths of computer paper and pin this up on the wall. You begin to see the work in its entirety and not just as a large number of single sheets. This makes it easier to reposition sections for better effect.

- Avoid sending out any letter containing an obvious correction. It makes the recipient feel they weren't important enough to warrant you re-typing the letter. Wordprocessors produce perfect copy and do away with the need for Tippex.

DESIGNING YOUR BROCHURE

Brochures are widely used to advertise business services. However, many homeworkers ignore their possibilities. This is unfortunate as a well designed and written brochure can be a terrific sales tool. The £80-100 spent on producing a brochure is money well spent. Many small firms make the mistake of trying to make their brochure appeal to all people. Such a blunderbuss approach all too often means that the target is missed completely. Before writing and designing your brochure you must answer a few questions.

- What do you want to achieve with your publicity? Do you want to increase new orders from old clients, or find new ones altogether?

- Who is your publicity aimed at? If you try and appeal to everyone then you will probably reach no-one.

- What is your unique selling proposition? This is the quality or feature that makes you different from other homeworkers in your field. For instance, are you promoting your quality, a very different type of service, the speed of your delivery or your reliability? Choose one idea as your main theme and keep the other ideas in the

Ideas That sell

Words That Work

1 Homend Hopkilns
Cradley
Malvern
Worcestershire
WR13 5NW
Tel/Fax: 01886 880532
Contact: Ian Phillipson

HOW TO PROMOTE YOUR BUSINESS

Dear

Over the years I've watched your company grow. You
have a knack of letting the world know you are
around. Your company literature and appearances in
magazine and television features certainly show you
as a business that knows the value of good
publicity and promotion.

But I think that there are some other cost
effective ways in which you could make a stronger
impact to win more business.

The opening of this letter is strong and different. It
praises the company and indicates a long-term interest
in their business. The next section is important
because it suggests that they can do more to raise their
profile, without directly `knocking´ their present
promotional company. It also drops the hint that if the
company will miss out if they don't respond. As it
happens they didn't and they did.

Professional publicity you can afford

Fig. 8. The opening paragraphs of a 'cold call' letter promoting the
services of the publicity company, Ideas that Sell.

background. Make yourself different from everyone else. Most people put out a brochure that is boring. Make sure that yours isn't.

• What personality do you want your brochure to have? Check this against your list of business qualities.

When you send out your brochures don't expect the world to come rushing to your door. The response to mailouts is generally low. A 5% response rate is considered extremely good.

Action point
Make a collection of brochures from your competitors. What are their good points and their bad points? What can you learn from them?

USING THE TELEPHONE TO EXPAND YOUR BUSINESS

The telephone is a valuable sales tool for anyone in business. Knowing how to use it means that most homeworkers can improve and develop their business without leaving their desk. It is also your lifeline to the outside world. If you work a lot on the phone then it is worth learning how to use it effectively.

How to be professional on the phone
Every time the phone rings take the attitude that the person on the other end is about to offer you a million pound deal which will evaporate if you don't sound as professional as you can be.

You can either answer the phone with your business name, if you have one, or simply give your name in a friendly but business-like manner. This gives the impression that the caller has come through on a direct line.

Never respond to a call by giving just your number. It makes you sound definitely residential and creates totally the wrong impression. ICI or Ford don't answer business calls with a 'Hello this is Blenkinsop 123'. Make sure you don't either.

During office hours *you* should take all calls whenever possible. The rest of the family needs to understand that these could be the very calls that pay for their food, holidays, cars and diamond necklaces, and as such all are potentially important. If others do answer the phone, make sure that they give no flippant responses of the 'Hello, Battersea Dogs Home' variety.

Young children should never answer the phone during work hours. Even if you are just the creative or organisational genius a client is looking for, they will find it off-putting to encounter a lisping six-year-old acting as your receptionist. Should such a situation occur, use humour to defuse the situation. Some joke about that being 'the real managing director'

Ideas That sell

Words That Work

1 Homend Hopkilns
Cradley
Malvern
Worcestershire
WR13 5NW
Tel/Fax: 01886 880532
Contact: Ian Phillipson

HOW TO PROMOTE YOUR BUSINESS

Dear

For any new business, advertising seems the obvious way to let
customers know you're around. For High Street fishmongers it's
not a bad starting point, but for many other businesses, it can be
a hit and miss affair, bringing poor results nearly always at
great expense. Not the best way to promote a young company.

There are other ways of working the media and market to your
advantage. Take these routes and you really pin up your company's
name before your clients' eyes ... cost effectively.

It's early days for your company, I know, but I'd like to do some
promotional work for you. Basically anything to do with words
or promotional ideas we do. That includes PR, press releases,
brochures, leaflets, mailshots and advertising.

As you'll see from the enclosed material we have a strong background
in publicity and promotion. Some clients have been 'big boys',
while others have been small companies, or often one-man bands,
and no worse for that.

Your idea has a strong buyer appeal. You'll succeed with or
without our help. But I do think I have ideas and promotional
skills that can shift your business profile up more than a few gears.
If you'd like to talk then give me a call, I'd be happy to tell
you more.

Yours sincerely

Ian Phillipson

Professional publicity you can afford

Fig. 9. Shows a letter to a new company. It takes a somewhat different
tack, but both are highly personalised letters aimed at one person.
They do not use the standard devices of a direct mail shot,
because that would look too manufactured.

might do the trick, and then move quickly on to business. Don't apologise profusely.

If there are likely to be such problems, then the only sensible solution is to subscribe to another phone line. Then you and everyone else knows that any call on this line is to do with work and should be treated accordingly.

How to get the most out of a call

- If you know the caller, picture them sitting in front of you.

- Pay careful attention to the tone of their voice and words. Are they happy, sad or angry? You should react accordingly.

- Concentrate on the call. You can't do something else and listen effectively at the same time.

- Be natural on the phone. Treat the call as though it were a face-to-face conversation. If you normally make a point by waving your arms around then do the same when you are on the phone.

- Smile as you talk. It makes you sound friendlier.

- Always stay in control of your emotions. Never make calls when you are angry. Cool down before dialling. If you become tense take a few deep breaths ... silently... and try some relaxation exercises.

- Don't be rushed into making decisions over the phone. If you need more time, ring back later.

- Strange though it may seem, the ear with which we listen affects our attitude to the conversation, according to British Telecom. To analyse complicated facts, put the receiver to your right ear. This communicates with the logical left side of the brain. To listen sympathetically, switch the phone to the left ear. This sends messages to the intuitive right side of the brain.

How to make difficult calls

Though these points apply at any time you make a phone call, they are particularly important when you are having to deal with late payers, official organisations and... bank managers.

- If you need to resolve a problem, don't wait for the other party to call. Phone them first.

- Stand up to make the call. It makes you sound more authoritative. Lounging in a chair makes you sound more relaxed.

- Always know what you are going to say before the call. Make notes before you dial.

- Get to the point of your call quickly.

- At intervals repeat points back to the other person so that you are sure you have understood what they said.

- If the other person has called, thank them for calling or the help. Such praise tends to encourage co-operation. You should include your caller's name in the last sentence as this ends the conversation by making them feel good.

- Repeat key facts in the last few sentences. This helps the other person remember them better.

- When you decide to end a call, be firm. Don't allow the conversation to start up again as you lose valuable time.

How to sell on the phone

There are two basic types of phone selling; the cold call and the warm call. Warm calls are easier because you use the recommendation of a friend or satisfied client to break the ice. If you do this, it is important to check that your 'reference' is happy for you to use their name.

If you don't have a mutual name to use as a reference, then you can still warm up your call by first sending a sales letter to your prospective client, waiting a few days before phoning up to see if they have received it.

Cold calls are made to prospective clients who don't know you from Adam. You 'go in cold' by having to explain about yourself and what you have to offer all at once.

Before you start selling on the phone, make a list of all the people you are going to call, their company names and their telephone numbers. Leave space to make notes of their responses and your future actions.

- Decide on a time when you are going to start your phone selling. Don't let anything distract you.

- Remember to smile while you make the call and keep smiling throughout. It makes you sound friendlier and relaxes you.

- Involve the prospective client in the conversation quickly by asking questions. This way you'll find out whether they are interested in your business.

- Don't ramble. You will quickly lose your prospective client's interest and avoid long pauses as these make you sound unenthusiastic and unprepared.

- Don't just chat to people. Know what you want to achieve before you make the call and try to achieve that, e.g. get an appointment or win an order.

- If your client is negative, don't just say 'thank you for listening'. This is your chance to start selling. If you have worked out a sales script before the call then you won't be flummoxed by a rejection. Every business requires a different sales script, but most work on similar principles.

This is part of a sample telephone script for a homeworker who trains people in the use of computers.

(Homeworker to switchboard) 'Hello, could you tell me who deals with the computer training for your staff?'
(Switchboard) 'That would be Mrs Dawson.'
'And what's her Christian name?'
'It's Dorothy.'
'Thanks. Would you put me through please?'

(At this point, the caller could call back later, asking for Dorothy Dawson, not Mrs Dawson, which suggests she knows her. This gives more authority, rather than looking as though you are on a 'fishing trip'.) The call could then go something like this.

'Dorothy Dawson please.'
'Speaking.'
'Hello Mrs Dawson, my name's Ian Phillipson. I hope I'm talking to the right person, you do organise the computer training programme for your staff don't you?'
'Yes.'
'That's great. Well I work for Keyboard Systems and we specialise in providing computer training for companies in your industry. Tell me, do you do all of your training in-house?'
'Yes we do, it's cheaper than using someone from outside and we can rely on the quality.'
'But, if I could show you that we could offer you the quality of training that you're used to and do it cost-effectively would you be interested?'
'Well I suppose so.' (It would after all be illogical for Mrs Dawson to say anything else.) At this point the caller should be able to arrange a meeting. However, if Mrs Dawson says 'No', then the caller will have to do more selling.
The key is always to find out why the potential customer is saying no. Is it because they don't use your services? Are you seen as too expensive, inexperienced, or small to do the job? The homeworker must find out and counter this shortcoming by emphasising the benefits of using Keyboard Systems.

Nine rules to improve your tele-sales

1. Make sure that you talk to the right person—someone who can make decisions.

2. Act like an actor when you are selling on the phone.

3. Never be underhand when you call a potential customer. Tell them who you are and what you want. Never pretend that your call is personal if it is not.

4. Work hard on the first 20-30 seconds of your sales script as this is when you have to really capture your listener's attention.

5. Leave pauses in the script when the customer can make comments.

6. Don't sell too hard. Use an opening phrase such as 'Can I have just sixty seconds of your time to tell you about...?' Very few people will refuse you this.

7. Sell yourself, your products and services with word pictures that bring your sales talk alive. When you have written it out, record yourself giving the script. Now, how can it be improved?

8. Give your prospect alternatives. Rather than saying 'which day of the week would suit you best for a meeting?' say, 'would Monday or Tuesday be better for you?'

9. If someone tells you 'no' find out why. If you can't sell to them, it might help counter the same argument from someone else.

Case history – Steve scans the local press

Steve is an architect working from home in a small country town. Every week he takes the local newspaper and reads it from cover to cover looking at planning applications, business people's plans for the future, reports on council meetings and the letters page. When he finds a story on a project that he thinks could use his services he writes a sales letter to them, following up with a phone call a few days later. By 'advertising' in this way, Steve keeps his promotional costs down—postage and the time he spends reading the paper are his only costs.

WHEN A CLIENT COMES TO CALL

There may be times when you have to see a client at your home, either through necessity or at their wish. If that's so, never desperately try to dissuade clients from seeing you there. If you do they are likely to become suspicious of you and wonder what you have to hide. Should that mistrust go too deep then you might find yourself without that client.

When you work from home, careful and early preparation is the key to a successful client visit.

- First, decide where you are to hold the meeting. Your office will be the best meeting place if you need to illustrate points with the computer or use the telephone, but it is not always the best place. If your office is small and cramped, without comfortable seating, or is in an inaccessible part of the house, then meet in the 'best room' in the house. This will probably be the living room, though if a large table is required it may be the dining room.

- Make sure you have enough space, chairs and materials readily to hand. It is inexcusable to waste your client's time and your own by having to hunt for information. At the very least your client will think you inefficient.

- If it will help, use a flip chart to display your information, or a large layout book propped against a chair.

- Fifteen minutes before the client arrives, switch on the answer machine. You do not want to be 'trapped' on the phone by a talkative, but important supplier some minutes before the doorbell chimes. And leave the answer machine on during your client's stay. If you can regulate how quickly the phone is picked up by the machine, set this to the shortest time possible so that the phone does not ring for long.

- When your client arrives, never apologise for seeing them at your home. This is your working environment—the working environment of a professional—so act confidently. Show them into your office or the room you have chosen for the meeting and have tea, coffee and cups or mineral water ready to offer.

- When clients come to see you it is a business call, not a social one. They are there to discuss work. They expect an uninterrupted session, so once your meeting has begun there should be no disturbances from other members of the family.

- Make sure your family knows the importance of the meeting. If the meeting is very important, children should be out of the house. With the best will in the world they do find it difficult to keep quiet, and if a baby has to bawl, then he or she has to bawl. In even the most informal business meetings this is distracting.

  If you show that you are constantly being disrupted by noise, the client may be put in two minds. The last thing you want to do is put doubt in your client's mind about your ability to do the job.

- For the same reason, cats and dogs should be banished before your client arrives and for the duration of the visit. Even if your client is an animal-lover, hairs and claws can make a mess of an expensive suit. Make sure that there are none on the chair your client is to sit in.

- If a problem such as noise or another interruption does occur, deal with it promptly and quietly. Don't ignore the situation, but try and defuse it with some humour. Even if you are annoyed by a disturbance, never become bad tempered, which is easier to do in the relaxed atmosphere of your own home.

- Throughout your meeting, stick to business. Though meetings held in such relaxed conditions are often highly productive, the relaxed surroundings can encourage you to chat away to your clients as though they had just popped round for social chit-chat. Be careful.

- The time to show off your prize fuchsias in the garden, or the Picasso on your bedroom wall is after the meeting. But in this, let your client take the lead. Don't railroad them into a tour of inspection.

Action point

1. Make a list of the prospective clients you could sell your services to by phone.
2. Write down every benefit clients would receive from using your services, and of every objection they could make should they not use you.
3. Using the above devise a telephone sales script for your products and services.
4. If you don't think that you can sell yourself then think about employing someone to do it for you. Ask around for someone who is in sales and may be willing to do freelance work for you.
5. Alternatively, book yourself on to a sales course for small businesses. Your local TEC should have details. And begin reading books on sales techniques. Make sure that when you learn something new about selling you take the time and trouble to employ and practise that technique.
6. Look at ways of marketing yourself to obtain bigger and better contracts, for instance by teaming up with a fellow homeworker who has complementary skills and pitching for larger contracts that you wouldn't otherwise win working on your own.
7. Keep a very close eye on your marketing efforts by developing a Marketing Log. This simply is a document on which you record every sales letter, tele-sales call, and marketing meeting that you have. It will help you set marketing targets for yourself which you can aim for each week or month. When working for yourself and by yourself it is very important that you keep a close eye on your marketing efforts so that you are marketing regularly.

11
Working to the Future

SPOKEN FROM EXPERIENCE

'The future is something which everyone reaches at the rate of sixty minutes an hour, whatever he does, whoever he is.' C S Lewis.

'If you would like to hit the mark you must aim a little above it.' Longfellow, poet.

'Many hands make light work.' Proverb.

'Too many cooks spoil the broth.' Proverb.

'Retirement at sixty-five is ridiculous. When I was sixty-five, I still had pimples.' George Burns, veteran comedian.

'I don't want any yes men around me. I want everybody to tell the truth, even if it costs them their jobs.' Sam Goldwyn.

DO YOU NEED TO EXPAND?

If you are successful with your homeworking business, then at some point your requirements are likely to change. When this happens you will have to carefully examine your future ambitions.

If you need more space, then the most cost-effective solution is simply to move from one part of the house to another. If you do not have a spare room you will have to swap with another member of your family. If this isn't possible then you could consider converting an outhouse or garage into your office. This is a more expensive route to take and may require planning permission.

The standard garage will require a lot of additional insulation on walls and roof if you are to stay warm and cosy in the depths of winter. The floor will also have to be improved. Concrete is not the best surface to stand on all day. You can either cover this with a cushioned floor covering, or lay a floor of boards over the top of it. You are also likely to require additional lighting and some form of heating. Then of course you have the problem of where to put the car!

If you don't have a garage or don't want to take up the space, then look upwards to your loft. Most spaces can be converted using the services of a specialist loft conversion company, or a good builder.

Both will work to your specifications and incorporate features that you think are most useful in your office. It may be best not to make the area too specialised since in future years you may want to use it as an additional bedroom. You could also put off potential buyers of the house who just want to use it as living, and not office space. Depending on the alterations you want to make, planning permission may be needed.

With no space in the house or the garage, then a well insulated building in the garden could provide the solution. Garden buildings are quickly erected, within weeks rather than months, as they come in sections and stand on a concrete platform.

Homelodge is one company that produces a number of garden buildings that can be used as office space and provide very comfortable and convenient working conditions. Large glass windows flood the office with light, while heaters can be pre-set to warm the office up, for you to start work in warmth, not winter cold. Installation, lighting, power points, carpeting, heating and internal and external decorations are all part of the package with prices starting at around £10,000.

The fact that the office is separate from the house can also prove an added attraction for those who need the motivation of leaving the home and 'going out' to work.

If you are short of office space then the most drastic action may be to move house. Some houses are now being built which actually take into account the activities of homeworkers, and have been wired with extra telephone and fax lines. You may find that your business really takes off, and then you may have to move your business out of the house and look for office space elsewhere!

Action point

Ask yourself the following questions about your present situation. If you answer yes to most of them, then home may no longer be the best place for you to work from and it could be time to move.

- Do you need additional equipment which cannot be fitted into your present office?

- Is your present office needed for another purpose, a nursery perhaps?

- Can you afford to make a move elsewhere?

- What would be the benefits of making a move?

- What would be the disadvantages of making a move? It would certainly be less convenient, but what else do *you* need to consider.

- Are you going to employ more than one person on a regular basis?

When strangers are trooping in and out of the home day in day out, it can soon become a strain on the other members of the family who can see their presence as an intrusion into the home.

- Are more and more customers and suppliers coming to your home? Remember that your neighbours have every right to complain if you are causing them a nuisance with your activities.

- Do you need to make your business more impressive? Big deals can be clinched from a home office, but sometimes a 'proper' office is what a client wants to see.

FINANCING YOUR BUSINESS

If you are looking to expand your business, by taking on more staff, increasing the size of your home office by converting part of your home or adding to it, or to solve a short-term cash flow problem, banks and building societies are likely to be your first port of call, but there are other sources of funds that may help you. In nearly all cases, your accounts will be vital in convincing lenders that you are a good risk and a worthwhile venture to back.

The Loan Guarantee Scheme

For those in business who cannot offer adequate security for a loan, or would otherwise find it difficult to raise finance, the Loan Guarantee Scheme can provide sums of money up to £100,000. This scheme reduces a bank's risk of lending money as 70% of the loan is guaranteed by the Government. DTI Loan Guarantee Scheme, Level 2, St Mary's House, c/o Moorfoot, Sheffield S1 4PQ. Tel: 0114 597308/9.

Help for the disabled

Grants for equipment and training are available to disabled people who wish to run a business. Also for an initial period, weekly grants are also payable to employers who take disabled staff. Your local Jobcentre can put you in contact with the Disablement Advisory service who can offer help.

Business Start-Up Grants

Until a few years ago The Enterprise Allowance Scheme provided a means of encouraging people to set up their own businesses, by giving them a regular income for the first year of business. This national scheme has since been overtaken with start-up grants and aid being provided on a more local or regional basis. To find out what is available in your area contact your local Training and Enterprise Council, Business Link or Job Centre.

Rural Development Grants

A small business that is operating from parts of rural England, or towns with populations of less than 10,000 may be eligible for loans from the Rural Development Commission. Not all business types are eligible for funding, for example professions such as accountancy and solicitors, and retailing, apart from sole village shops, are exempt. Marketing and exhibition grants are also awarded to help small businesses achieve profitable sales.

EMPLOYING STAFF

There are four main reasons why you will need staff:

- to do work that you don't like doing
- to do work that you can't do
- to take over some of your workload
- to free time for you to do higher paying work.

What do you want staff to do?

Before you invite anyone to an interview you should be very clear about what you want your staff to do. Otherwise how can you choose the best person for the job when even you don't know what you want them to do?

Checklist

- Do you want them to do the filing, answer the phone, the typing or a bit of everything? If it is to just answer the phone then a pleasant voice is essential, but for filing a clerical background would be helpful.

- How well trained do you want them to be? There is no point hiring a highly professional and expensive secretary if a bright school-leaver could do the paperwork in your office.

- How many hours a week are you expecting them to work? Are they to be full-time or part-time? Many people are willing to work part-time. You could in fact create a job sharing scheme with several part-timers coming on different days of the week. This would allow them to work to their lifestyles.

- Where will they work? In your office or elsewhere, perhaps even their own home?

- How much extra equipment are they going to need and how much is it going to cost you? Would it be better to look for staff who have their own equipment, such as a wordprocessor?

- Will you supply them with lunch, will they go out to eat or will they bring their own food? What about snacks and coffee?

- Will you give them a door key? If you do, are they going to have it just for the day, the week but not weekends, or all of the time? What about when you go on holiday?
- Will you want them to work while you are not there?
- Will they be your 'employees' or will you be using them on a freelance or casual basis? This affects not only their status and dealings with the tax man, but also yours.

Where to find staff

With today's levels of high unemployment there are many good quality people looking for work. First of all, look close to home for your employees if you only want somebody part-time. Perhaps your husband, wife, girlfriend or boyfriend could do the few hours of work you need done each week? If they can't be persuaded to help, or don't have the skills or the time, then ask your friends if they could spare time, or know someone else.

Trying to find such connections is not a waste of time, because you are not just looking for someone with certain skills, but someone you can also trust. Otherwise you will be inviting a total stranger into your house. A positive recommendation from a friend about someone they know, while no guarantee of their honesty and nature, should at least give you an indication of a person's character.

Should you recruit staff that are unknown to you, then always ask for references and be prepared to take them up. Use the phone to do this, it is faster and the people you talk with will probably be more informative and open than if you just wrote a letter.

On a more formal basis, your local Jobcentre, Careers Service or training scheme should be able to send you candidates for your job. Alternatively you can place an advert in the local newspaper or even put a card in a shop window advertising the position.

Action point

- Write a short job description of the kind of person that you want to hire. Include in it the main activities you want the person to perform and the skills that are needed to do this.
- Write out a second list of additional skills which it would be useful for your staff to have. Then if your business takes a change in direction you know that your original employee will be able to cope.

How to help your staff perform better

Good relations with your staff are crucial if both you and they are to be able to work effectively together.

- Keep your staff busy. People hate being bored, especially if you have chosen someone who is bright and enthusiastic.

- Involve them in your business. They will work more efficiently and you will be able to delegate some of your workload to them.

- Once you have asked someone to do a job, let them get on with it. You only irritate and slow them down if you are always changing your mind or checking up to see how they are doing.

- Give them work as early in the day as possible and preferably the night before so that they are ready for an immediate start in the morning.

- Trust them. This won't be a problem if you have chosen the right person in the first place.

- Check that the person you are taking on actually can do the main job that you want them for. Even though they may have certificates, give them some documents to type as part of the interview, if that's what they are being employed to do. Don't stand over them while you do this but disappear for fifteen minutes or so and make allowances for the fact that they might not be used to your wordprocessing system or typewriter.

- Set ground rules with employees at an early date. What areas of your house are they going to be allowed into? You would presumably want to keep your bedrooms as a no-go area, but are you going to let them use your kitchen to make coffee?

Your legal obligations to staff

When you take on staff you must comply with certain legal requirements. Your obligations include informing the tax office when they start working for you and when they leave. You must also calculate and pay appropriate tax and National Insurance contributions if they become your employees rather than freelance staff, who are responsible for their own tax and NI. Inland Revenue leaflet IR53 outlines the basic tax requirements that you should bear in mind.

Within 13 weeks of starting work, an employee is entitled to a 'Statement of the terms of employment'. This should be a highly comprehensive document covering all points of employment. Even if you just take on a single part-timer you should send them a formal letter of employment which gives details of the date they will start work, their hours, their rates of pay, holiday arrangements, method of payment and any other relevant matters.

Once employed it is always dangerous to simply dismiss staff as you may be liable for claims of unfair dismissal. A leaflet about unfair dismissal is available from the Employment Service or a local job centre. This should give you a good idea of what you can and cannot do.

Detailed compendiums, such as *Croner's Reference Book for Employers*, give accurate details of employees' rights, unfair dismissal and sick pay.

Tax and your staff

If you pay someone believing them to be self-employed, and they are not, then you are in trouble. For you are responsible for deducting their PAYE payments, and if you don't you may have to pay that sum to the Inland Revenue at a later date. Your only defence is that you made the mistake in good faith.

To avoid the problem, you should make a careful check about your potential employee's tax status. Ask for a letter from their accountant declaring that they are self-employed. If you cannot obtain that, then ask for their tax reference number. The number for the self-employed consists of three digits divided by a slash from five others, for example 123/45678. If you are in doubt then ask the Inland Revenue.

Case history – Samantha's down-time

After three years' trading, Samantha's design business is going well. She works about sixty hours each week charging £20 an hour for her time, which should give her a weekly income of £1,200. However, Samantha spends twenty hours each week on paperwork that's essential but doesn't earn her any money. This down-time effectively loses £400 from her potential earnings. Her income is now only £800 a week.

To help her solve the problem Samatha employs a friend's daughter to do her filing and correspondence. This costs her £5 an hour—£100 a week for the twenty hours.

Admittedly Samantha's regular bills now go up, but she uses the 'extra' twenty hours she has created to earn another £250 a week on average. Employing clerical help means that she effectively increases her net income by £150 a week.

Case history – Jon employs a pensioner

Jon also wanted to get some help in his home office, but for a different reason. For while his basic business working as a management consultant was going very well, he was keen to expand into other areas. He had lots of ideas for new businesses, but just not the time to find out the information necessary to see if they were viable. What he needed was in fact a research assistant. He thought this might make a very interesting part-time job for an intelligent college, even school-leaver or perhaps during their holidays. He talked to a few people he knew who suggested some likely candidates. Jon tried out several of these but encountered the same problem. For while bright in themselves and often well-qualified, these youngsters needed too much direction and help. What Jon was asking them to do was so outside of their experience. They didn't last long. There was just no point in Jon employing someone when he ended up doing the job all himself. In the end, after a little lateral thinking, Jon went in completely the opposite direction by employing a pensioner who loved finding things out and used to be a librarian. This whole episode taught Jon two things.

First, even though you might think what you are asking someone to do is relatively simple, really think about whether it is, particularly if you want people to be 'self-starting'. Acting on your own initiative is as much a skill as anything else.

And second, think about finding the right person for the job, even if they don't spring to mind as obvious candidates in the first place.

Glossary

Anti-climb paint: Paint which makes drainpipes slippery to climb and therefore helps keep burglars out of your home office.

ASCII: American Standard Code of Information Interchange. A common way of ensuring that information is interchangeable between computer software. You should ensure that any wordprocessing software you buy can convert its files into ASCII format (or another 'universal' format) and that it can read ASCII files.

Baud rate: The speed at which a modem sends and receives information.

Buffer zone: A way of separating your home office from the rest of the house. This is a way of ensuring that you don'ts confuse social time with work time.

Call analyser: Device that helps you monitor and analise the telephone calls you are making.

Call Diversion: A telephone service that diverts callers to your number to another number.

Call recognition: A telephone service that identifies the number of the person calling you before you answer.

Call Return: A telephone service that lets you find out who has called you by dialling 1471.

Call Waiting: A telephone service that tells you when a call is coming in when you are engaged on another, giving you the chance to break off.

Cold calling: Phone calls to prospective customers or clients with whom you have had no dealings before.

Covenant: Restriction on the deeds of your house which may limit the kind of work that you can do from there.

Data Protection Act: Legislation that controls and limits the amount of personal information that can be held on computers about individuals.

Database: A large electronic store of information which can be accessed using a computer and modem. Alternatively a database is a form of software that lets you hold information in a convenient form on your computer.

Day Book: A book which becomes the central reference point for information in your home office.

Deadline: A time or date by which you intend to have completed a certain task or part of it. Deadlines are useful in motivation.

E-mail: Or electronic mail, is a means of sending messages and information quickly and easily. Now becoming almost a must for anyone working in a home office.

Floppy disk: A disk of either 3½ or 5¼ inch diameter which fits into the computer. You can read and write information on to it.

Footprint: The area on the desktop that a computer takes up.

Goal: A target that you set yourself. Important in self motivation.

Hard disk: A large magnetic storage disk held in the insides of a computer. You can never have too much hard disk storage space.

Hardware: A collective name for computer equipment. Not to be confused with software.

ISDN: Integrated Services Digital Network. A telecommunications system that allows you to send not only voice, but also data, fax and video. It is a very fast method of transmission.

Magic Hour: Specific time set aside to achieve certain tasks.

Mailshot: A planned mailing of letters and other promotional material to prospective customers.

Mercury: A rival telecommuncations company to BT.

Modem: A box of electronics that converts signals from your computer into a form that can be sent down the phone line to another computer. Likewise the modem can convert signals sent to it down the phone line from another computer elsewhere.

Netiquette: Network etiquette, or the proper way to express oneself when using e-mail.

QWERTY: The standard layout for a keyboard.

RSI: Repetitive strain injury. A painful condition that can occur in those who spend long hours at the keyboard.

Salami technique: The chopping up of a large job into smaller pieces so that it becomes more manageable.

Software: The opposite of hardware. These are the programs that the computer hardware needs to perform functions such as wordprocessing and accounts work.

Stress: Excessive tension that can lead to health problems.

Target: The same as a goal.

Telecottage: Or telecentre, a community centre filled with equipment such as computers, printers and e-mail, where people can come to telework or use the facilities.

Teleworking: Employing computers and the telephone to send, receive and process information.

Time log: A tool to assess your productivity.

Time management: The efficient organisation of time so that you get more done in a given period.

VDU: The visual display unit or monitor of your computer.

Virtual company: Teams of people who can be located anywhere in the world, who work together on particular projects. They may never ever meet physically, instead just passing information and knowledge between them down the phone lines.

Virus: A malicious program that can damage your computer's hard disk. Passing on a virus is illegal under the 1990 Computer Misuses Act.

Wordprocessor: A software program that allows your computer to operate as a very powerful and sophisticated typewriter.

Workaholism: The desire to keep working all hours.

Useful Addresses

GENERAL BUSINESS MATTERS

The Association of British Chambers of Commerce, 9 Tufton Street, London SW1P 3QB. Tel: (0171) 222 1555.

Business Link. Tel: (0800) 104010 (for business support services).

Federation of Small Businesses, 32 Orchard Road, Lytham St Annes FY8 1NY. Tel: (01253) 720911.

Prince's Youth Business Trust, 5 Cleveland Place, London SW1Y 6JJ. Tel: (0171) 321 6500.

LEGAL AND FINANCIAL MATTERS

Finance and Leasing Association, 18 Upper Grosvenor Street, London W1X 9PB. Tel: (0171) 491 2783.

Lawyers for Enterprise. Tel: (0171) 405 9075. These are solicitors who will offer a short, free initial interview concerning the general points you should consider when setting up or running a business.

Law Society, 113 Chancery Lane, London WC2. Tel: (0171) 242 1222. The solicitors' professional body.

Office of Fair Trading, Field House, Bream's Buildings, London EC4. Tel: (0171) 242 2858.

Tolson Messenger, 148 King Street, London W6 0QU. Tel: (0181) 741 8361. Offer special insurance policies to people who work from home.

PRESENTATION AND PROMOTION

The Advertising Standards Authority (ASA), 2 Torrington Place, London WC1E 7HW. Tel: (Offers fast, free and confidential copy advice on your advertising and promotions by telephoning (0171) 580 4100).

Companies Registration Office, 55 City Road, London EC1Y 1BB. Tel: (0171) 253 9393.

Companies Registration Office, Companies House, Crown Way, Cardiff CF4 3UZ. Tel: (01222) 388588.

National Business Names Registry, Somerset House, Temple Street, Birmingham B2 5DP. Tel: (0121) 643 0227.

Registrar of Companies, 21 Bothwell Street, Glasgow G2 6NL. Tel: (0141) 248 3315.

Ideas that Sell, 1 Homend Hopkilns, Cradley, Malvern, Worcestershire WR13 5NW. Tel: (01886) 880532. Offers advice and help to homeworkers who want to promote their business.

SELF MANAGEMENT

Successories Ltd, 2 Aspen Units, Aspen Way, Yalberton Industrial Estate, Paignton, Devon TQ4 5BR. Tel: (01803) 666111 (motivational posters etc).

CareerTrack International, Drayton Road, Newton Longville, Milton Keynes MK17 0DY. Tel: (01908) 366544 (suppliers of self-improvement seminars and tapes).

Nightingale Conant, Unit 10, Mitcham Industrial Estate, Streatham Road, Mitcham, Surrey CR4 2AP (self improvement tapes).

Wyvern Business Library, 6 The Business Park, Ely, Cambridgeshire CB7 4JW. Tel: (01352) 665544 (supply a range of business and self improvement books).

New World Cassettes, Paradise Farm, Westhall, Halesworth, Suffolk IP19 8BR. Tel: (01502) 79279 (self improvement tapes with subliminal messages).

HEALTH AND SAFETY

The Association of Optometrists, Bridge House, 233 Blackfriars Road, London SE1 8NW.

The Chartered Institution of Building Services, Delta House, 222 Balham High Road, London SW12 9BS.

The RSI Association, Chapel House, 152 High Street, Yiewsley, West Drayton, Middlesex UB7 7BD.

VDU Hazards Factpack (£6.00) and *An Office-Worker's Guide to RSI* (£4.00). City Centre Project, 32/35 Featherstone Street, London EC1Y 8QX. Tel: (0171) 608 1338 (RSI and general health matters involving computers).

TELEWORKING

The Telecottage Association, The Other Cottage, Shortwood, Nailsworth, Gloucestershire. Tel: (01453) 834874.

National Association of Teleworkers. Tel: (01404) 47467.

Message Direct (24 hour answering service). Tel: (0800) 132050.

CIX. Tel: (01492) 641 961.

CompuServe Information Service, 1 Redcliffe Street, PO Box 676, Bristol BS99 1YN. Tel: (0800) 289378.

Demon Systems Ltd (commercial Internet access in Britain) 42 Hendon Lane, London N3 1TT. Tel: (0181) 349 0063.

BBC Networking Club, PO Box 7, London W3 6XJ (provides low-cost access to the Internet.

EQUIPMENT

All Types Business Computers Ltd, Courtenay Park, Newton Abbot, Devon TQ12 2HB. Tel: (01626) 331133 (voice recognition systems that allow you to dictate direct to your computer).

The Back Shop, 24 New Cavendish Street, London W1M 7LH. Tel: (0171) 935 9120. Suppliers of ergonomically designed chairs, desks and computer tables.

For information on Network Services, such as Call Waiting phone BT by dialling 150 or to buy BT equipment phone (0800) 334422.

Ikea, Drury Way, 255 North Circular Road, London NW10 0QJ. Tel: (0181) 451 5566; Europa Boulevard, Warrington. Tel: (01925) 55889; Park Lane, Wednesbury, West Midlands. Tel: (0121) 526 5232. A source of good quality low-cost benches, tables, chairs and lights.

Mercury Customer Services, PO Box 49, Birmingham B1 1BR. Tel: Frecall (0500) 500 194.

Intercom (Mercury 'smart sockets'). Tel: (0800) 626474.

Small Business Campaign Desk, Mercury Communications Ltd, PO Box 3132, Birmingham B2 4BR. Tel: (0500) 700100.

SECURITY

Hamber Safes, Radford Way, Billericay, Essex CM12 0EG. Tel: (0277) 624450.

Andura. Tel: (01869) 240374 or Bitumastic. Tel: (0191) 483 2321 (anti-climb paint).

Circle Security market The Minder security locking plates. Tel: (01527) 374858.

Newcom Services market The Wobbler (electronic equipment protection). Tel: (01903) 374858.

Tolson Messenger Ltd, 148 King Street, London W6 0QU. Tel: (0800) 374246 (home office insurance).

COMPUTER SOFTWARE, SUPPLIES AND ACCESSORIES

Akore Shareware, Freepost, Nottingham NG1 1BR. Tel: (0800) 252221.

Misco Computer Supplies Ltd, Subscription Department, FREEPOST,

Wellingborough, Northants NN8 6BR. Tel: (01933) 400400.
SELTEC, Britsel Data Services, Albert House, 10 Albert Street, Bournemouth, Dorset BH1 1BZ. Tel: (01202) 559 199 (shareware).

OFFICE SUPPLIES

Neat Ideas, Sandall Stones Road, Kirk Sandall Industrial Estate, Doncaster, South Yorkshire DN3 1QU. Tel: (0800) 500 192.
Officepoint, PO Box 67, Wetherby, West Yorkshire LS23 7XW. Tel: (01937) 841414.
Office World. Tel: (01345) 444 700.
Viking Direct. Tel: (0800) 424 444.
Paperback (green stationery), Unit 2, Bow Triangle Business Centre, Eleanor Street, London E3 4NP. Tel: (0181) 980 2233.
The Green Stationery Company, Studio 1, 114 Walcot Street, Bath BA1 5BG. Tel: (01225) 480556.
Paper Direct, FREEPOST (LE296) Hinckley LE10 0BR. Tel: (0800) 616244.

PROBLEMS

National Childminding Association, 8 Masons Hill, Bromley BR2 9EY. Tel: (0181) 464 6164.
National Council for One-Parent Families, 255 Kentish Town Road, London NW5 2LX. Tel: (0171) 267 1361.
Pre-School Play Groups Association, 61-63 Kings Cross Road, London WC1X 9LE. Tel: (0171) 833 0991.
Professional Association of Nursery Nurses (PANN), 77 Friar Gate, Derby DE1 1BT. Tel: (01332) 43029.
Working Mothers Association, 77 Holloway Road, London N7 8JZ. Tel: (0171) 700 5771.

GARDEN OFFICES

Homelodge Buildings, Kingswell Point, Crawley, Winchester, Hampshire SO21 2PU. Tel: (01962) 881480.

WATCHDOG ORGANISATIONS

Consumers Association. Tel: (0171) 486 5544.
EEA (the Association of the Electronic, Telecommunications and Business Equipment Industry). Tel: (0171) 331 2000.
Office of Fair Trading. Tel: (01742) 892345.
Trading Standards Department, see your local telephone directory.

Further Reading

BUSINESS MATTERS

A Guide to Working from Home, British Telecom Guide.
Be Your Own Boss, British Telecom Guide.
The Business of Freelancing, Graham Jones (BFP Jones 1987).
How to Start a Business From Home, Graham Jones (How to Books, 3rd edition 1994).
The Wyvern Business Library, Wyvern House, 7 The Business Park, Ely, Cambridgeshire CB7 4JW. Suppliers of a wide range of business books, available through mail order.

LEGAL MATTERS AND TAXATION

Computers and the Law, David Bainbridge (Pitman 1990).
Law for the Small Business, Patricia Clayton (Kogan Page 1991).
A Step by Step Guide to Planning Permission for Small Businesses available from your local authority planning department.
Tax for the Self-employed (Allied Dunbar Money Guide), David Williams (Longman 1990).
Taxman Tactics, How to play by the rules – and win, Stephen Courtney (Sidgwick and Jackson 1990).
Your Business and the Law, John Harries (Oyez Longman).

HEALTH

Fluorescent Lighting and The VDU Hazards Handbook, London Hazards Centre, Third Floor, 308 Grays Inn Road, London WC1X 8DS.
How to Beat Fatigue – put more zest into your life naturally, Louis Proto (Century Arrow 1986).
Lighting for VDUs, The Chartered Institution of Building Services, Delta House, 222 Balham High Road, London SW12 9BS.
A Manager's Guide to Self Development, Pedler, Burgoyne & Boydell (McGraw-Hill 1978).

Office Yoga, Julie Friedeberger (Thorsons 1991).
RSI Association, c/o Christ Church, Redford Way, Uxbridge, Middlesex UB8 1SZ.
Stress Management Techniques, Dr Vernon Coleman (Mercury Business Books 1988).
VDU Hazards Fact Pack, Health and Safety Executive.
Working with VDUs. Free leaflet available from The Health and Safety Executive.
Your eyes and VDUs, Association of Optometrists, Bridge House, 233 Blackfriars Road, London SE1 8NW.

DESIGN

DIY by Design, Terence Conran (Conran Octopus 1989).

ORGANISATION AND TIME MANAGEMENT

Conquering the Paper Pile-Up, Stephanie Culp (Writer's Digest Books, Cincinnati 1990).
Getting Things Done; The ABC of Time Management, Edwin C. Bliss (Futura Publications 1976).
How to Manage an Office, Ann Dobson (How To Books 1995).
Running your Office, Margaret Korving (BBC 1989)
The Seven Keys to Superefficiency, Winston Fletcher (Sidgwick & Jackson 1986).
10-Minute Time and Stress Management, Dr David Lewis (Piatkus).
101 Ways to Clean Up Your Act, Dianna Booker (Kogan Page).

EQUIPMENT

A Guide to Office Waste Paper Schemes, Friends of the Earth, 26-28 Underwood Street, London N1 7J. Tel: (0171) 490 1555.

PRESENTATION AND PROMOTION

Don't Get Mad, Write, Bruce West (Kogan Page).
High Income Consulting, Tom Lambert (Nicholas Brealey).
How to Do Your Own PR, Ian Phillipson (How To Books 1995).
How to Do Your Own Advertising, Michael Bennie (How To Books 1990).
How to Increase Sales by Telephone, Alfred Tack (The Windmill Press, Surrey 1971).
How to Promote Your Own Business, Jim Dudley.
How to Publish a Newsletter, Graham Jones (How To Books, 2nd edition,

1995).

How to Write a Press Release, Peter Bartram (How To Books, 2nd edition, 1995).

How to Write a Report, John Bowden (How To Books 1991).

The Language of Success, BT booklet.

101 Ways to Get More Business, Timothy R V Foster (Kogan Page).

The Secrets of Effective Direct Mail, John Fraser-Robinson (McGraw-Hill, London 1989).

The Secrets of Successful Copywriting, Patrick Quinn (Heinemann, London).

The Secrets of Successful Low-Budget Advertising, Patrick Quinn (Heinemann, London 1987).

Seductive Selling, Kit Sadgrove (Kogan Page).

Total Confidence, Philipa Davies (Piatkus).

Write Right, A Desk Drawer Digest of Punctuation, Grammar and Style, Jan Vernolia (David & Charles, London 1982).

Writing to Sell, The Complete Guide to Copywriting for Business, Kit Sadgrove (Robert Hale, London 1991).

Writing to Win, Mel Lewis (McGraw-Hill, London 1987).

COMPUTER BOOKS

I Hate Buying a Computer, Jim Felici (Que).

Buy a PC, Mike James (I/O Press).

Beginners Guide to the PC, McKellan and Waixel (Kuma Books).

COMPUTER MAGAZINES

Computer Shopper
PC Plus
PC Direct
Practical PC
The Computer Buyer
The Internet
Micro Computer Mart
.net
What PC?
What Personal Computer

TELEWORKING

Home is where the office is, Andrew Bibby (Hodder & Stoughton).
Technology Tools for your home office, Peter Chatterton (Kogan Page).

Teleworking: A strategic guide for management, Steven Burch (Kogan Page 1991).

Teleworking Explained, ed. by Mike Gray, Noel Hodson, Gil Gordon (Wiley-BT).

Telework: Towards the elusive office, U Huws, W B Korte & S Robinson (John Wiley & Sons, Chichester 1990).

Telecommuting: How to make it work for you and your company, M M Kelly & G E Gordon (Prentice Hall International, Hemel Hempstead 1986).

The Telecommuters, F Kinsman (John Wiley & Sons, Chichester 1987).

Remote Office Work: Implications for individuals and organisations, M Olsen (School of Business Administration, New York University, 1981).

The Sunday Times, Teleworking video.

The Whole Internet User's Guide and Catalog, Ed Krol (O'Reilly & Associates, Inc).

YOUR FAMILY AND YOUR BUSINESS

The Working Woman's Guide, L Hodgkinson (Thorsons 1985).

The Working Woman's Handbook, Edited by Audrey Slaughter (Century 1986).

Womanpower, Penny Perrick (W H Allen 1983).

The Good Nanny Guide, Charlotte Breese & Hilaire Gomer (Century 1988).

Picking the Perfect Nanny, Jane P Metzroth (Pocket Books 1984).

RECRUITING AND EMPLOYING STAFF

How to Conduct Staff Appraisals, Nigel Hunt (How To Books, 2nd edition, 1994).

How to Employ and Manage Staff, Wendy Wyatt (How To Books, 2nd edition, 1995).

How to Manage People at Work, John Humphries (How To Books, 2nd edition, 1995).

Index